Great Dads & Grandfathers

Great Dads & Grandfathers

George Durrant

spring creek
BOOK COMPANY
Provo, Utah

ISBN: 978-1-932898-71-2
e. 1

Published by:
Spring Creek Book Company
P.O. Box 50355
Provo, Utah 84605-0355

www.springcreekbooks.com

Cover design by Nicole Cunningham

Printed in the United States of America
10 9 8 7 6 5 4 3 2 1
Printed on acid-free paper

Library of Congress Cataloging-in-Publication Data
Durrant, George D.
Great dads and grandfathers / by George Durrant.
p. cm.
ISBN 978-1-932898-71-2 (pbk. : alk. paper)
1. Love, Paternal. 2. Father and child. 3. Grandfathers. 4. Family--Religious life. I. Title.

HQ756.D79 2007
248.8'421088289373--dc22
2007008127

TABLE OF CONTENTS

DEDICATION

To my dad, Bert,
who was a great dad,
and to my eight children,
who deserved a great dad,
and who gave me the opportunity
to be a grandfather.

Love at Home
Starring Father

AUTHOR'S NOTE

The fact that you are willing to read this book indicates that you realize that "there is beauty all around when there's love at home."

I realize, as do you, my fellow fathers, that a mother is most often the heart of the home. But almost all great productions call for a leading man.

I invite you to try for that role. And if you try and pray and love, you'll get the role—you'll even be the star!

Chapter 1

THE HONOR OF BEING A FATHER

Greetings, my fellow fathers. Can you think of anything as magnificent as being a father? As far back as my memory will reach I recall having a longing to become a father. I dreamed of sometime finding a beautiful wife, establishing a home of our own and filling that home wall-to-wall with children. I suppose that one reason this desire for fatherhood was so strong in me was that I, being the youngest of nine children, didn't have the joy of having younger brothers and sisters.

I had a friend and neighbor whose name was Herbie Pawloski. He was the middle child of a family of eleven. When I visited Herbie and his family, I'd see all the little children there and I'd become a bit jealous of him. At Christmastime my envy would be most intense. I had become too old to get toys and so had Herbie. But because of his little brothers and sisters, on Christmas morning his house was still filled with toys and mine was not. I could hardly bear such inequality.

Perhaps this was one of the reasons I had an intense desire to grow up and become the father to a whole flock of little children. I could envision no greater thrill than playing with my children and with their Christmas toys (the ones I had always wanted) and to hear them call me "Daddy."

To accomplish my family dream, I had to wait those long years until I was fully ready for this, the greatest of all responsibilities. As time passed my desire to become a husband and father became even stronger. When those rewarding two years of missionary life ended, I felt ready, with the Lord's help, to make my dreams come true. The exciting search for my future wife was intensified.

I found a girl who loved me as I loved her. I asked her to marry me and she accepted. In the temple we became eternal partners.

A few months after our wedding, I came home from my labors to assist my wife in preparing our evening meal. As I peeled the potatoes with a paring knife she was nearby opening a can of peas. The words she spoke on that great moment in history I shall never forget, for it was my single most fulfilling moment. She said, "I went to the doctor today. We are going to have a baby."

Her words almost put me into a state of shock. I had to quit peeling the potatoes—my hands trembled with such excitement that the task became too dangerous to continue. My heart pounded within me. I jumped up and down with glee. I delicately hugged my wife. My dream was coming true. I was going to become a father. I wanted to shout the news to all the world.

As the time for the baby's arrival came closer, I was drafted into the army and stationed in Arkansas. I had to live on the base while Marilyn lived in town some twelve miles away.

The army doctor told us that when she came to the base hospital to have the child I'd be notified so that I could be there. But on the night of the birth I was not notified. The next day I stood outside the army mess hall in a line waiting for the noon meal. Someone came to me and said, "Durrant, you are to call the hospital." I crossed the road to a phone booth and called.

The nurse announced to me via phone the long-awaited magnificent message, "Private Durrant, you are the father of a fine baby son."

Tears of joy filled my eyes. I bounded out of the phone booth with the agility of a great athlete. I half ran and half jumped along as I shouted to my soldier friends who had known that the event was near, "I've got a son! I've got a son! I'm a father! I'm a father!" Even now as I recall these memories I feel excitement surging through my soul. My buddies cheered for me as I quickly ran the few blocks to the post hospital, my mind filled with thoughts of joy. I felt like pinching myself to make sure I wasn't involved in a dream. But I knew it wasn't a dream. It was true. I was indeed a father. I recall thinking, as I neared the hospital, "I'd like to light a new star in the sky to announce the arrival of my son." Nothing short of that seemed adequate to express how happy I was.

I dashed into the hospital and down the hall. As I went along I saw the glass windows of the newborn baby room. I stopped and looked in. There among the three or four little ones was a baby whose crib bore the name Durrant. As I looked my whole soul tingled with a spiritual thrill. This was my son. And I was his father.

I went to Marilyn's room. She seemed more beautiful than ever. As we talked of all the wonders of what had happened, I excitedly said, "That little boy—he looks just like me."

She squeezed my hand as she said, "I know that, but let's keep him anyway."

Thus our firstborn was delivered to us in an army hospital. The cost was just eight dollars. He's been worth every cent of that—plus a million dollars more.

I know that you as a father could tell quite a story about the arrival of your first child. I'm sure you agree with me when I say there's no experience like that which comes at the time when a husband and wife can say, with joy, "Unto us a child is born."

Our second son was our third child. At the time I was teaching seminary in Brigham City, Utah. It was my birthday. I was called to the phone. Marilyn, who was close to the time of delivery, said, "I believe I have a special birthday present for you. Come home and let's go to the hospital to get the gift."

I excitedly told the students, "Teach yourselves," and away I went. Soon we were at the hospital. She went to be prepared for the birth and I went to the father's waiting room.

A half-hour or so later I was reading a magazine when the doctor interrupted me by asking, "Would you like to come into the delivery room?" His question rather shocked me and I replied, "Well, I would, but as you can see, I'm reading this *Sports Illustrated* magazine."

He replied, "Maybe you could read that later."

I stammered a little and said, "I'm afraid I would get a little woozy in there. I'm not too good at such things."

In kindness he said, "Come on in. Marilyn would like you to and I'm sure you'll do just fine."

I was out of excuses, and so I followed along, praying silently that all would be well.

What followed was the most unforgettable experience of my life. The doctor explained all that was happening. My heart was filled with the warmth of the Spirit of the Lord. I stood in awe as the baby was born. The doctor held him by his ankles and for a few seconds there was silence and then the baby cried. Seeing the baby and hearing his first cries caused a sensation in my soul that was more than my emotions could bear without tears. I cried too. I've never seen such a miracle. Certainly birth is indeed the most glorious and wonderful of all events.

With these two births, and six others equally as thrilling, we have been blessed to receive from heaven eight choice spirits who have become part of our family. To some people eight children seems like a lot but to others it is but a few. As one great man once said, "Some have eight or nine children. That's their business. But as for my wife and me, we like a large family." They had fifteen.

Fathers have families of different sizes. But whether our families are one or fifteen we rejoice in the thrill of fatherhood.

To be co-creators with our beloved wives is an honor that goes beyond all other honors and a responsibility that dwarfs all other responsibilities. Being trusted by our Heavenly Father to receive one of his own spirit children is a most divine opportunity, and to prepare that child to someday return to his or her heavenly home is a responsibility beyond description.

As I think of the honor of fatherhood, I recall that at work I was once asked to fill out a questionnaire. One of the questions was, "What honors have you received?" I thought as I read the question, "I'll leave this question and come back to it."

I filled in all the other blanks and then again looked at the words, "What honors have you received?" I could think of none. I'd never been all-state in anything nor had I been elected to any office. I felt a little unimportant as I left the item blank. I folded the paper and placed it in the envelope for mailing. But before I sealed it, I paused. I took the paper out of the envelope and smoothed it on the table.

I picked up my pen. In response to the question, "What honors have you received?" I wrote the glorious words, "The Melchizedek Priesthood." My soul was stirred as I considered again the honor and thrill of being an elder. But having written that, I now knew that I must write more. I then recorded another honor—I wrote the word "Husband." It's such a joy to be a husband and to strive to be worthy of the honor of having a woman love and respect you. Having listed these two supreme honors, "Melchizedek Priesthood" and "Husband," I was now inspired to list my final and greatest honor. I wrote with reverence the sacred word, "Father."

So my honors were listed: Melchizedek Priesthood, husband, and father.

Such honors when seen with eyes that really see make the honors of men shrink and hide in the wings.

It's a humbling experience to address this book to all who share with me the sacred title of Father. As someone has said and as we firmly agree, there is no word which describes a higher title, for it is by the name Father that even God has chosen to be known.

I, as you do, tremble a bit as I consider the awesome task of filling the role of father. I take comfort in two things: (1) We have to take things only one step at a time, and (2) God, our Heavenly Father and the Heavenly Father of our children, will help us and make us equal to the responsibility.

I recall a story that came out of World War II and which I saw depicted in an old movie. In the story a navy pilot during the early days of the Pacific campaign had been quickly elevated in rank due to the fact that many of his superiors were killed in the intense struggle. Finally this young officer became aware that he would soon be asked to become a commander of many other pilots. He knew that in that role he would have the almost unbearable responsibility of directing men to places from which they would never return.

He was called before the admiral, knowing what he would be asked to do. He decided to refuse the command. As he had suspected, the orders were that he take the assignment. In response he quickly refused on the grounds that he was not qualified. The admiral arose from his chair, came around the desk, and put his hand on the young man's shoulders.

Looking into his eyes, the admiral said, "What do you want me to do—find a great man for this terrible responsibility? Well, let me tell you something. There aren't any great men. There are only great responsibilities. When ordinary men like you and me meet a great responsibility, and fulfill it, then a great man is born."

And so, my fellow fathers, I know that we can do it. We can receive a newborn child and we can fulfill the responsibility of being the kind of father that child deserves. As we meet with faith and with love this mightiest of all responsibilities, we can become great. For there is none so great as he whose deepest desire is to be a good father.

Along the way problems will arise, as they did for the great prophet and father, Lehi. Sometimes we will suffer heartache, as did he. But through it all, if we continue in our righteous desires, our children will say of us, as Lehi's could of him, "Having been born of goodly parents, therefore I was taught in all the learning of my father."

Chapter 2

A PRIESTHOOD FATHER AND AN ETERNAL FAMILY

Fathers in the Church are different in many ways. Some of us are plumbers, some carpenters, some physicians, some teachers, and some cowboys. Some like poetry and bird watching; others like hunting and raising roses. Some read hundreds of books, many only the sports page. Some can use words the way an artist uses his brush; others find it difficult to express themselves.

But there is a common element that gives fathers in the Church equal potential in a most important area. That common element is the Melchizedek Priesthood.

Fathers in the Church can hold this power, which gives them the right to act in the name of the Lord, to preside over their families and raise their children in his name.

When you became an elder you were given a power that gives you, more than can education or other qualification, the capacity to succeed as a father. If you aren't yet an elder you can and you should become one. You need to be an elder. Your family needs you to have that power. If someone left your family a one-million-dollar inheritance it would never be as significant to you and your wife and your children as would the blessing of your becoming an elder. Children need and deserve to be loved, disciplined, and taught by a father who holds the holy priesthood and who thus has the power to do those things in the name of God.

The following incident happened to me and members of my family. (The story has been used in other Church contexts.)

It was Sunday afternoon. We had all been to Sunday School and now the time approached for sacrament meeting. My young son, who felt that he had had enough church for the day, asked, somewhat negatively, "Dad, are you going to church again tonight?" I quickly replied, "I sure am."

His next question was, "Why?"

Wishing to teach him a lesson on the importance of church attendance, I paused to bring into my mind the best possible answer.

While I needed a little time to think, it seemed that my nine-year-old daughter Kathryn didn't. She spoke right up. In response to the question of why I was going to church again, she said with conviction, "Because Dad is a priesthood man, that's why." Her answer both shocked and thrilled me. My eyes moistened with tears as I considered the truth which she had so quickly and simply stated.

As I sat there I found myself thinking, "A priesthood man—why, that's better than being a Harvard man or a Princeton man, or any other kind of man." "I'm a Priesthood man," I said silently. It sounded good. What an honor and what a joy it is to be a priesthood man!

And the place to be a priesthood man is at home. Children need a priesthood man for a father. He doesn't have to be a college graduate, or be high-salaried, or be dashing and handsome. He doesn't have to be in the limelight in the world or at the chapel. All he has to be is a priesthood man; then he's equal to any man, regardless of background or prestige.

A high school building custodian worked five days a week under the direction of the high school principal. Because the principal served under the district superintendent, we could say that the custodian served under him also. The state superintendent of public instruction has some authority over all schools and so in a small sense he too was considered a boss of the custodian.

It happened that the custodian, the principal, and both the district and state superintendents all lived in the same ward. The custodian was the high priests group leader and the three school administrators were all high priests in his group.

Thus, once each month these three school officials came to the custodian, whom they directed at the school, to report to him in personal priesthood interviews their priesthood stewardships and to receive from him direction in their Church duties.

This case doesn't show that one man is better in any setting than another but it does show that the priesthood is the great "uncommon denominator." It makes men who are different in many ways equal in the most important of all ways.

A man whose soul is tempered and strengthened by the priesthood has the inward promptings that make him equal with the best of fathers. A "priesthood man" calls his family to family prayer. He calls upon someone to ask a blessing on the food. He calls them together for family home evening. He goes to Church with his family. He prays with his wife. He pays his tithes and offerings. He prays for divine guidance in all things. In his own way he teaches and loves his wife and children. He brings unnumbered blessings to his family.

Give your family the supreme gift of being led by a priesthood man. As a priesthood man who honors his ordination, you will be a blessing to your family and love will abide in your home. You will lead "by persuasion, by long-suffering, by gentleness and meekness, and by love unfeigned;

"By kindness, and pure knowledge . . .

"Reproving betimes with sharpness, when moved upon by the Holy Ghost; and then showing forth afterwards an increase of love toward him whom thou hast reproved. . ." (D & C 121: 41-43)

Yes, we fathers are different in many ways. But through the priesthood we become magnificently alike. A king in the Book of Mormon promised God in prayer, "I will give away all my sins to know thee." (Alma 22:18)

As fathers, we should be willing to say, "I'll give up anything I possess or do whatever I must if I can have the priesthood and can be worthy to use this power to bless my family."

Among those things that might be given away in this wonderful swap are cigarettes, beer, dirty jokes, Sunday recreation, dishonesty, and a multitude of other spiritual roadblocks. In return you can receive the power of the holy priesthood. What a deal!

A friend of mine made just such sacrifices to receive the holy priesthood. I hadn't seen this friend for years when he approached me on the Brigham Young University campus where I worked. We had once been close friends, but after high school we had gone our separate ways. Mine had led me to Church activity, a mission, and a temple marriage. His way led him away from the Church and all its blessings.

He said, "I knew you worked here and I've wanted to see you. As you know, I didn't go to college after high school, but now I've finally decided to get an education."

I responded, "That's great. What classes are you taking?"

He replied, "Well, I'm really only taking one class because I can only go at night, and this is my first semester here."

I asked, "What's the one class you are taking?"

His reply thrilled me, for he said, "Well, I decided I'd take the most important class that is taught here."

I asked, "What's that?"

"It's the Book of Mormon." He seemed to sense that I was a bit surprised. He quickly added, "I've changed some in the past few weeks. Last week I became an elder, and next month my wife and my three children and I are all going to the temple to be sealed together as a family."

He went on to tell me how he'd given up smoking, drinking, and many other things in order to become worthy. Tears filled his eyes and mine as he said, "Life sure is a lot better now. Finally, we've found what real happiness is." He then had to hurry off to class.

My friend had given away so little and had gained so much.

By being worthy priesthood men, we provide a channel through which the Lord will pour out blessings beyond measure to our families.

A man who in worthiness holds the Melchizedek Priesthood holds the power to succeed as a father. A man who holds not this power cannot succeed as an eternal father no matter what else he possesses.

Some years ago, while pursuing a graduate degree, I conducted a study on the subject of family home evening and its influence upon children. To carry out the research, I located a number of families who had seldom, if ever, held family home evenings. I visited these families, who were quite inactive in the Church, and asked them if they would conduct a family home evening each week for a period of three months. I advised them that I felt that by doing so it would help their children have more self-confidence. To measure the effects of the home evenings on the children, I asked the parents for permission to give their children a "self-image test" both before and after the three months.

Twenty-five families agreed to the experiment. Interesting things happened as they carried out this program.

I shall forever remember one family's experience. When I went to this family to make my original request, I found a ruggedly handsome father, a beautiful wife, and five young children. The home was lovely and well kept. Upon my arrival in the home, that father put his smoking pipe aside and talked to us in a most cordial way. A can of beer was open near the side of his chair. As we spoke of several subjects, I learned that he refereed high school basketball games. Thus we had a common interest—sports.

Finally I told him the purpose of my visit. I made the request, and he accepted, saying that he would faithfully conduct a family home evening each week. His wife and family seemed pleased at his response. I gave them a few guidelines to follow, administered the self-image test to their children and told them that I'd visit them again in three months.

Winter had nearly turned to spring before I saw them again. I called them by phone and made an appointment to come to their home. As I was greeted by this family, I felt almost overwhelmed by their welcome. We visited for a time and then I asked, "Well, did you do it? Did you have a home evening every week for the past three months as you said you would?"

The father looked at me intently and said, "I'm not sure. Most weeks we did, but there was one week we aren't sure if what we did was a family home evening or not."

I was pleased at their faithfulness and said, "Well, if you had one every week but one, that's pretty good."

The mother then said, "I think we could even count what we did that week. Anyway, we wanted to ask you if what we did would count."

I said, "Tell me what you did and we'll see."

The father replied, "That's the week we went to the temple to be sealed together forever as a family." His eyes were moist with tears as he asked, "Can we count that?" I was caught off-guard by this unexpected response and I could hardly speak because of emotion. I softly replied, "Yes, I believe we could count that."

The mother's eyes and face shone as she said, "We went to the temple on my birthday."

He quickly added, "I couldn't even get her much of a present. Since we started paying tithing, there's not money left over."

Tears fell freely from his wife's face as she looked into his eyes and said, "When you took me to the temple, that was the best present that I've ever received because that's what I wanted more than anything else in the world." By now the children all wanted to tell me about the temple and what going there meant to them. After listening to their happy reports, I asked the father, "What happened to cause this mighty change?"

His simple reply was, "Well, I did what you said. Each week I'd call my family together and we'd have family home evening. After a few weeks, I saw the children sitting there real close to me and their mother. We all felt so good and so happy. I just decided it was time we started changing things. We talked about going to the temple so that we could be together forever. We talked to our home teachers and then to the bishop. And in a few weeks we felt we were worthy to go to the temple."

The pipe that had lain smoking by the father's side three months before was now gone, and so was the beer can. Things had changed at that house. What had been given up had been replaced by something too beautiful to describe. This father, like my high school friend, had made the wisest of all trades when he had put aside his sins and gained the blessings of being the priesthood father of an eternal family.

If you are one of those fathers who has not yet taken your family to the temple, put your life in order so that you can take them in the near future. And to those whose wedding ceremonies were performed in the temple, be forever careful to keep alive the glorious promises that were given us there.

All fathers—be they tall, short, fat, thin, white- or blue-collar workers—have the power to give their families this precious gift. Our Heavenly Father cares little about our way of honorably earning a living. His only concern is how we live. Let's live as priesthood men and preside forever in the most basic and lasting of all organizations—the family.

CHAPTER 3

TIME AT HOME

When my three-year-old daughter said, "Gladasicanbee," to me as I came home one night, I thought she was giving a strange name to her new friend. But then I understood as she put things in proper context by singing, "I'm so glad when daddy comes home, gladasicanbee." Thinking back on her words causes me to realize again that when daddy or father comes home, he comes to the place where he matters most. And what a blessing it is when all the family can sincerely say that they are glad that daddy is home.

When you come home from work or anywhere else, you have left a place where you are of lesser importance and have entered a place where you are of far greater importance. At your place of work, you are needed. But, sad as it may seem, there has never been a man who, when he leaves his daily job for another or when he retires, is not adequately replaced; things go on quite well without him.

As one man said, "I felt that if I left the company, it would take a month or so and then I'd be replaced and they wouldn't even miss me. But," he said, "I was wrong. It only took a week." Likewise, a man's golfing, hunting, bowling, and fishing partners all like his company, but even they could carry on quite well if he were not there.

But there is a place where a man has no substitute. Not after a month or a year or a generation. That is the place where they call him "Father." When he leaves home, he's missed. And until he returns, there will be an empty, unfilled space in the hearts of his family. It is undeniable. A man's greatest contribution is made in his home with his family.

Let us therefore be fathers first and everything else second. Let us put a good effort into our work and even a better effort into our families. Let us be guided by the gentle truth that tells us our work never has nor ever will be as important as our family. True, we must earn a living, and we must do our best in our labors, but if an undue amount of time is spent earning a living, then there is a likelihood that the living we earn is not the type of living that will bring us joy.

We long ago decided in our society that to be a clockwatcher at work is not admirable. However, if a man works with vigor while he watches the clock, then perhaps it's not so bad. Especially if, when work time ends, and there are no pressing matters at work, he almost runs out of the office or plant, jumps in his car, and heads happily for home.

I for one love to leave work right on time and hurry home. I suppose the reason for this is that I'm more popular at home than I am at work. When I get home I hear all kinds of requests: "Dad, play ball with us," or "Dad, come and see this." Oh, what a joy it is to come home!

Perhaps you are a businessman. Long hours are required of you or the business could fail. Often the necessity of spending long hours at work occurs when your children are young.

It's easy not to be home because they don't seem to miss you. But those young years are crucial. Set goals and pray that your business might reach the point where you can spend more time at home.

Some fathers in the economic crunch of the times work two jobs. It's eight hours on one job, then off to another. This may seem the only way to make ends meet. But if this is done to purchase things that could be done without, we make a great mistake. Our children need our time more than they need any less important luxuries.

Church work often sends us out and away from home. But, by setting proper priorities, planning, and delegation, we can organize ourselves to be effective in Church duties and to be home much more often than we would suppose.

Some fathers who spend undue amounts of time at work or in Church callings take pride in these long hours away from home, which they feel is a mark of dedication. Perhaps it is dedication, but in too many cases it is just a way of not going home.

Some feel more confident and capable away from home than they do with their families. We should examine ourselves to see if, under the guise of "dedication," we've left to our wives the most important of all causes to which we should be dedicated—our families.

Some feel that if they devote many hours to their Church duties, the Lord will compensate by caring for their families and ensuring that all will be well at home. This does not appear to be as valid as we hope. Faithful Church men can and do have critical problems at home, one cause of which may be a lack of father-family experience.

On the other hand, we can reverse this idea and say that a reasonable amount of quality time spent with our wives and our children will bring us added blessings and power in fulfilling our Church callings. By being effective fathers and loving husbands, we feel good about the most important aspect of lives—our families. The father who feels successful at home comes out of that home filled with the spirit of love. His heart has been warmed by the home fires of his own family. He is then able to go forth and warm the hearts and souls of his brothers and sisters. A man who is happy and well-loved at home and who is dedicated to the Church receives the Spirit of the Lord. It is that Spirit which brings success in Church work.

So let's all go home whenever we possibly can. And until we can go home, let's think about the time when we can. The most uplifting thought that I can invite into my mind is the thought which says, "Pretty soon I'm going to go home."

While serving with the army in Korea, I was away from my wife and son for a year. I had many reasons to become discouraged. When on guard duty or some other difficult task, I felt as if the world was quite a crushing place to be. But then my thoughts would turn to Marilyn and my little son, who were thousands of miles away. It would warm my whole soul to think, "Very soon I'll be going home." That thought kept me going all that lonely year. But even if you've been gone only since seven o'clock that morning it is still uplifting to think of your family, to smile and say to yourself, "Very soon I'll be going home."

There will never be a journey as important as the one that takes you home. Go home as often as you can and as early as duty will allow. Spend both quality and quantity time at home—both are essential. Some of us fathers know that we are not home enough, and we say to ourselves and to others, "It isn't the quantity but the quality of time that a father spends at home that matters." There is truth in this statement, but we must not let it be a salve to a conscience that says we are too much away from the family.

When I was called to be a mission president, I was fearful that at a most critical time in the lives of my eight children I might not have sufficient time to be a good father. I was determined that being a father was a more important call from the Lord than being president. That meant that even though I would dedicate myself to the mission, I would double my dedication as a father. I knew that in order to preside effectively in the mission, I must first preside well at home. I spent much time with my family, knowing they were the only ones who would still be mine at the end of my mission. If they felt secure and happy in the early days of our mission, things would go from good to better.

One of the first orders of business was to throw a big rope over a high limb on the huge ash tree that towered over our front yard. An acrobatic elder climbed the rope and tied it to the limb. Thus the giant mission home swing was born. With the swing came instant neighborhood friends for our younger children.

A few months after our arrival, we attended a mission presidents' seminar. Each president, asked what he felt was his best idea so far, reported on some program which he felt had enhanced the work. When my turn came, I said, "The best thing I've done so far is to build a swing." Everyone laughed. Elder S. Dilworth Young, a member of the Seventy who supervised the missions in the area, was amazed and asked, "What?"

I described the swing and explained that my major goal was to be a good father. I told of a young wife who had visited me just a few days before and had said, "My experience as a mission president's daughter was a nightmare from which I shall never recover."

I felt the Lord had sent her to me to teach me to look first to my family and then to the mission duties. The swing became my symbol of this setting of priorities. Later came a basketball standard and a sandpile. Our yard became a park where I spent much time with my children and where they settled for three happy years. I believe they will forever remember with joy their time in Kentucky and Tennessee.

May it so be that your children will often have cause to sing with sincerity, "I'm so glad when daddy comes home, Gladasicanbee."

CHAPTER 4

HELP YOUR CHILDREN FEEL GOOD ABOUT THEMSELVES

The way a child feels about himself is called his self-image. If he has good feelings about his self-worth and about his ability he will do well in life. Feelings of self-doubt will cause him many problems. Research has shown that the way a young child feels about himself determines to a large degree how well he will do in school and in life. Each child is born with certain limits to his learning abilities, but these built-in limits are seldom reached. The degree to which the child approaches these limits is based upon his inward feelings about his abilities.

We fathers play a vital role in our children's feelings about themselves. We serve as a sort of mirror for a child. When our children do something, they look to see our reaction. From what they see and hear and feel from us, their fathers, they begin to form opinions of themselves.

The way a child feels about himself, then, is in a large measure determined by the way his father reacts to him. Schoolteachers, bishops, Scoutmasters, coaches, and others often play important roles in a child's life, but none of these will ever be as important to a child's self-image as is his father. The father and, of course, the mother are the mirrors that the child uses in his early years and then consistently all his young life. From what he sees in his father's eyes and reactions, the child comes to feel either confident or unconfident, capable or incapable, accepted or rejected, loved or unloved. The child forms his feelings about himself in the earliest years of childhood. He or she is most blessed if in these young days an understanding father is near as often as possible.

All you've really got to do to help your children see themselves as being of great value is to praise them. Let them know that you feel they are capable and special. Sometimes we are too critical. We are too impatient. If only we could learn to praise more and criticize less! It would do so much to enhance the self-image of our children.

A statement such as "I'm sure proud of you—you really know how to draw good pictures" can be worth more to a child than a new bike. The bike will someday be gone, but the child's feelings about himself are eternal. Let your conversations with your children be filled with genuine and sincere praise. Children need to hear messages such as these:

"That was a good prayer."

"You sure are a big help."

"I'm really glad that I'm your dad because I sure like you."

"It's fun to go places with you."

"You and I are friends."

"You can do it if you try and I'll help you."

"You got fifteen out of twenty words right. That's good. Let's work on the others."

Let your child know without a doubt that you have confidence in him. Then when he goes to school, he will feel that he wears a price tag which says, "I'm a product of great worth." He will feel that he can do those things that the school experience demands, such as spelling, reading, and just plain fitting in.

If you criticize too often you can cause a child to feel he has little value. Statements such as "Did you do it wrong again?" and "You can't get anything right, can you?" damage a child and may cause permanent scars.

Avoid being a negative mirror that makes your child think he is a nobody. Eliminate from your relationship with him such statements as:

"I ask you to help and you end up making a mess."

"Go in the house; all you do is get in the way."

"I see you missed five words again. You're as dumb in school as I was."

"Quit bothering me; I've got things to do."

A child who is fed such a diet will soon see his price tag reading, "damaged goods," "soiled," "close out," "half price."

You can as a priesthood father control the things you say and do. It doesn't take more time, more education, more money. All it takes is a great desire to give your child the supporting praise and acceptance and love that his spirit needs as much as his body needs food.

Mathematically, your son or daughter probably does at least nineteen right things for every one wrong thing he or she does. Force yourself to give equal time. If you want to criticize the one wrong thing he did, comment on each of the nineteen right things. If children hear from you almost constantly what's right with them, when an occasional criticism is needed, it will help rather than wound them.

I've never seen my son Dwight happier than he was at a certain family home evening. He was five years old at the time, and a bit rowdy as I talked to the family. I was upset with him and said in a somewhat harsh voice, "Dwight! Come over here by me."

I believe he sensed that he might be in trouble. As he came closer I felt a bit of inspiration. "Dwight," I said, "you are a pretty smart boy so I've something for you to do. It will be hard, but I believe you can do it."

I then continued as all the family listened intently. "Dwight, I'm going to ask you to do some difficult things. I want you to go up those stairs. Go in my bedroom. Open the drawer where I keep my stockings. Get a pair of the stockings. Put them on the bed. Close the drawer. Go in the upstairs bathroom. Turn on the cold water. Turn it off. Come down the stairs. Go in the kitchen. Get a drink of water. Turn off the water. Come back in this room. Go up three stairs and back down. Come into this room and go around the chair. Then come over in front of me and say, 'Dad, I did it.'"

His eyes were opened wide with excitement as I asked, "Can you do it?"

Before he could answer, his older brothers and sisters tried to help by saying, "Dad, he can't do all that."

Dwight's expression indicated a feeling of excited confidence and I said, "Take off."

The house was silent except for the sounds made by Dwight. We heard his footsteps go up the stairs. The drawer was opened and closed. Then into the bathroom. The water on, then off. Down the stairs, past where we sat as he rushed into the kitchen, the water on, and then off. Back into the room and up three stairs and back down. Around the chair. And then, with his mission completed, he stood in front of me. He caught his breath and proudly announced, "Dad, I did it."

His brothers and sisters were amazed.

I asked him to come over to my side. I put my arm around his shoulders and pulled him close to me. I then said, "Dwight, you are really something. I'm proud of you. I'm so glad to be your dad. You are special."

His brothers and sisters said almost in unison, "Boy, Dwight! We didn't know you were that smart!"

He beamed until he almost glowed. I believe he'll never have another moment like that. Even if he were to someday stand on top of the winner's stand as an Olympic champion, he'd not feel as special as he felt in that room on that night with his family, and especially his father, singing his praises.

I believe that although he didn't realize it, he really felt as he stood before me, "I'm special. I can do things. People love me. I have great worth. I am a child of God."

For years after, Dwight would sometimes quietly say to me, "Dad, remember the night I did all those things? Can I do that again tonight?"

The joy that comes from feelings of self-worth can bring a child through the pain of the many tight places through which life forces him to pass. Therefore, the greatest lesson you'll ever teach your child will be that he is special. A child who feels his self-worth can say with conviction, "I am a child of God." Such are the seeds of success, and you as the father have the power not only to plant these seeds, but also to fertilize, to water, and to provide the sunshine of praise that will bring forth the happiness and success of your children as they sense their self-worth. And when you do these things, you'll have done much to fulfill your great role as a father.

Chapter 5

HAVING FUN WITH YOUR CHILDREN IS CHURCH WORK

If you were to ask one of my children, "Which would you rather do—ride on the roller coaster at an amusement park or wrestle with your dad on the floor at home?" they'd say, "Ride on the roller coaster." But that's just because they don't really know what they are talking about. They just imagine that they'd rather ride the roller coaster, but they'd really have more fun wrestling with me.

How do I know that wrestling with me is more fun for them than riding the roller coaster? Because I've seen it in their eyes and I've heard it in their voices. I've felt their feelings on both occasions. To me, the data is conclusive—a child's fun-barometer goes higher when he's playing with his dad than at any other time.

(And of course, wrestling, if you don't throw your back out, is so much less expensive than the roller coaster. This is another proof that the best things in life are free.)

Here I'm using wrestling with the children just as a symbol of all the enjoyable and exciting things there are to do with them.

A football game among themselves in the yard is exciting

for children, but when old Dad comes out and asks if he can be quarterback, then watch out. Supreme fun steps in and each child says, "Oh boy, this is great!" The only thing that dampens the fun is that Dad gets tired before the kids do and says, "I'd better quit." It's so difficult to see such fun end. Roller coasters fun? Sure, but not anywhere near as much fun as a football game with Dad.

When Dad steps up to the basketball court and says, "I'll take you one-on-one," his son's heart starts to pound. The father hooks in an old-fashioned shot and the son says, "Wow, Dad, you're back to your old high school form."

The father replies, "You haven't seen anything yet."

Again, the only thing to mar the fun is when the son says, "One more game, Dad?" and Dad, panting for breath, begs off with, "Maybe tomorrow. Right now [puff, puff] I've got some work to do."

A hunting or fishing trip with the world's finest big game guide isn't as much fun as a trip with Dad. One man who now holds a position of great authority once told me of his time spent in the mountains in late October with his father. "My dad's gone now," he told me with tears in his eyes, "but the memory of our hunting together will be with me forever."

He went on, "We'd make camp together. We'd hike the mountains together. We'd sit and wait for a buck together. And all the time we'd talk. He'd teach me what he held near and dear. In those times together, he gave me a desire to be and to do good."

The more he told me about those hunting trips with his father, the more emotion filled his heart as he said, "Those memories of my time with my dad are my most cherished memories."

But some of us aren't hunters or fishermen or athletes, so what do we do? The answer is simple. Do anything at all, and do it with the children. Anything they get to do with you when you are in a good mood is fun, even if it is work. Fixing a car, taking pictures, going to the state fair, training a dog, polishing rocks—anything that a father does with his children is fun.

That is, it's fun if the father sees that the children are more important than the activity. Take fishing, for example. A fishing trip isn't as much fun if Dad's trying to catch a lunker as it is if Dad's desire is to see the children catch even a small fish. When Dad helps them learn to fish, smiles and laughs at their tangled lines, unhooks their snags and, to a degree, acts crazy, the kids will have a ball. If the father can sort of let himself go and recapture the fun of being a boy, the children are guaranteed fun beyond measure.

You don't have to be an expert to do things with your children. Each year that goes by, my once all-American ability (in my mind, not the coaches' minds) wanes more and more. Now when I take the court against my sons it isn't quite as much fun for me as it was when I used to win. Now I sort of have to direct my efforts toward winning the sportsmanship trophy. I'm not very good any more, but that isn't really a factor. All that matters is that the children would sooner play with me than with the Globetrotters.

While you are at home, then, take time to play with the children. Take them places and do things with them. Many of us in the Church are busy men, and sometimes playing with the children is low on our list of priorities. I've found that I get more time in with my family if I keep reminding myself that playing with the children is Church work. I guess I'm just oriented to the idea that Church work has to be done. So when I consider playing with the children as being Church work, then I get it done.

While I was mission president, I would quite often resolve that it was again time for some more high-priority Church work. Then we would all go to an amusement park called Opryland in Nashville, Tennessee. It is a beautiful park where groups perform country-western music. I know of few more pleasant places. I just walked around the park with a smile on my face, holding hands with my children, eating all the cotton candy I could stand.

Once in a while, a thought would enter my mind: "Hey, you're the mission president. You'd better get back to the office." But then I'd smile again and say to myself, "Well, I'm doing my Church work here. I'm with my children and my wife. We're having a fun day and tonight I'll be able to write in my journal that I did six hours of glorious Church work today." I'd eat a little more cotton candy and let the children lead me wherever they wanted to go.

Church work with your family doesn't mean you leave other Church work undone. It merely means that you do both—and you can do both. Some days you can spend a whole day with the children. Other times it will have to be a ten-minute wrestle or one paper airplane constructed between dinner and the evening meeting. A few minutes of informal fun with Father every day makes a million memories for the children.

Some years ago, when we lived in Salt Lake City, we located a store where we could get ice cream cones for five cents. That price fit our pocketbook, so at least once a week all ten of us would climb in our station wagon and head for the store. We were so happy you'd have thought we were headed for Disneyland. A discouraged look would cross the waitress's face as she saw us coming; she knew that ten cones were coming up.

On the way back home we sang as we ate the ice cream. (We rolled up the windows so that the police wouldn't hear us.) We sang "The Golden Plates," "Some Must Push and Some Must Pull," and all sorts of songs.

One night, as we returned home and parked in the driveway, I said, "All of you, when you get out of the car go up and stand on the porch." They all stood there and I stood on the sidewalk two steps below them. I told them to look at the stars for a moment and then we'd pray. I thanked the Lord in the prayer for our family and for the joy we all felt when we were together.

I suggest that those ice cream experiences were Church work.

I believe such experiences can do more than any other Church experience to help children decide to live in accordance with gospel teachings.

Reading this chapter may have caused you to reevaluate how much you play with your children. If you don't do it enough, perhaps you feel a little guilty. If you do, then you are not alone. There's so much to do and so little time. But guilt should motivate action. Resolve anew to do more Church work with the children.

Both you and I can do better. It's not a matter of money, but only of the right priorities. If you come home too tired to do anything but plop down with the newspaper and the kids surround you with, "Dad, let's play ball" or "Come outside and see this," learn to say, "Kids, give me fifteen minutes and I'll be ready." Then relax fifteen minutes, and ask the Lord for strength to do some great Church work. The Lord will give you strength because he blesses those who do his work, and his greatest work is the work you do with the little ones that he has sent to you.

My fellow priesthood fathers, let's have fun with the children. In the long run it will make all the difference.

Chapter 6

LISTENING TO YOUR CHILDREN

The mark of a truly wise father is not how well he can speak but how well he can listen. So often we wish we were more prepared to know what to say to our children and we don't realize that far more important is the ability to listen to them.

The most satisfying and helpful times I've ever spent with my children have not been those times when I have talked to them, but rather those times when they have talked to me. Consequently I've made a discovery that I believe is more vital than the theory of relativity. My discovery is a simple one and it is this: The only time my children have ever talked to me was when I was really with them.

Among the most powerful influences you can have upon your children is the influence you have when you listen to them and convey to them that you understand. Plan to be with your children enough that they can talk to you. Children who truly have the time to talk to their parents will seldom go far astray. For those fathers who feel a lecture now and then is the answer, I suggest that lectures be lessened and listening be increased.

Blessed is a child who has a mother who will listen, but more blessed is the child whose father will also listen. A father who will do the enjoyable kind of Church work that I mentioned in

Chapter 5 will have the opportunity to listen. When you have fun with your children they will talk to you. It won't be a "third degree" environment, but rather a relaxed time to talk and to listen.

I recall an experience I had while playing basketball with one of my sons. Each time I took the ball out of bounds and just before I started to play, I asked him a question. He seemed a bit unhappy and didn't want to talk. I asked, "What did you have for school lunch today?"

He replied, very negatively, "The same old stuff."

I asked, "What exciting things happened at school?"

His reply was a disappointed, "Nothing."

Then I asked, "What did you do in Physical Ed today?"

He brightened a little and said, "Hey, Dad, I did good in class today." That sort of primed the pump, and he started to talk. After that there was a lot of time between baskets. Most of the time we just stood on the court and watched the sun go down and talked.

After some time our conversation deepened. He said, "Dad, I just don't feel good about things."

I asked, "What's wrong?"

He said, "I just don't feel good about myself." I listened and he continued. "I don't like the way I look."

I kidded him a little and said, "I don't understand that. You look just like me."

He smiled and said, "You look all right, Dad. It's just that I wish I were bigger. I wish I looked more like an athlete." He went on and poured his heart out to me. And as he talked and I listened, I understood and we were as one.

Finally we heard a shout from the house that announced that dinner was ready. As we walked toward the house, I put my hand on his shoulder. I couldn't make him any larger or look more like an athlete. All I could do was listen. But somehow I could see that just talking had sort of relieved the pressure for him. His mood had changed. He seemed to feel better.

You and I are often willing to listen just long enough to think we understand the problem. And then we break in and tell the child just what he should do. Such solutions are not what the child usually wants. For example, if your son says, "Dad, I don't feel good about myself," you might feel impressed to say, "That's nonsense, you've got so much going for you. You're twice the boy that the other kids around the neighborhood are. All you have to do is quit feeling sorry for yourself and count your blessings. All right, son?"

The son says, "All right." But he doesn't mean it and he still hurts. And if he keeps hurting, trouble lies ahead. Your greatest aid to him is to listen, listen, listen, and then speak just a few of the right words. Not words to belittle his problem, but words of understanding and perhaps a suggestion or two.

But it's hard. Time is short, and advice, although he usually doesn't want it, seems just what your child needs. So you offer a few quick words of advice like, "Don't worry, son, things will work out. I've got to go. Cheer up now and we can talk again sometime." And away you go.

Usually children tell you their feelings only after discussions on some preliminary subjects. Discussions about cars, about the World Series, about schoolteachers, about the news are the preliminaries that lead to the main event when the child says, "Hey, Dad, I've sort of got a problem." When the main event comes, stop talking and do some listening. It takes time to get to the main event, but the more often you do, the more your children will receive the strength they need.

Once our family was on a month-long journey to Canada. We had been in the car for days and were together so much that the children began to get on each other's nerves. After the first week of the journey we stayed in a vacant house owned by a friend of ours. One morning I was shaving when my oldest son came in and announced, "I want to catch a bus home."

When I asked why, he replied, "I've looked forward to this trip for almost a year. But I didn't know then that I'd have to be around my brother so much. I just can't stand to be around him anymore. He makes life miserable for me. I want to go home."

I felt like saying, "Don't be ridiculous. You can't go home. Why don't you grow up? It's probably more your fault than it is his. Now get out of here and forget going home. Just quit causing trouble."

This might have been the correct answer, but it wasn't the right time for the right answer and, for once, I didn't give the so-called right answer. Instead I said, "Okay, let me finish shaving and we'll talk about it."

In a half-hour I asked both of the boys to join me in an empty bedroom. We sat on the rug in the middle of the room.

I said, "Tell me again, son, what you told me before." He went through the same speech as before. The younger brother listened intently, and as he heard more and more it seemed his heart would break. He started to cry. When the opening remarks were concluded, I turned around and looked into the tear-filled eyes of the younger brother. I asked, "What do you have to say?"

He replied as best he could through his tears, "I know I bug you a lot, but it's just that whatever game we play or whatever we do you always win."

The older brother quickly replied, "Sure I win—I'm better than you."

The younger brother then added, "I know that. But every time you win, I lose. And I get so tired of losing I can't stand it." Then he sobbed.

The older brother's countenance changed as he said, "Just don't bug me so much and things will be better."

The younger boy replied, "I'll try not to."

We talked—that is, they did—and I listened. The spirit of love came among us. The boys now could understand each other. The older boy was ready to go on with us, and our vacation was saved. Listening had done in a feeling and voluntary way what a lecture might have done in a forceful and mandatory way.

Family home evening is an ideal place to listen. When the children start to talk, don't be quick to move in with a lecture-type lesson. Let them talk. Find out what they think and how they feel.

Once I asked my family, "Now, do any of you have any problems you want to talk about?"

My son said, "Yeah, why do we always have carrots so often at dinner?"

I replied quickly, "Because they are good for you, that's why." And feeling a little upset at his comment, I continued, "I get so sick of you kids complaining about the food. You learn to eat what you get. Your mother is a great cook and I don't want any more said about carrots. Besides, if you don't eat carrots, how are you going to see at night?" I then asked, "Now that that is settled, do any of you have any other problems you want to talk about?"

"Yeah, Dad. What time will we be through?"

We can chuckle at such an experience, but unfortunately its humor comes from its realism. As fathers, we have to think about and pray about and forever work on our ability to listen longer and form judgmental opinions more slowly.

A different reaction to the carrot criticism might have opened the door to discussion of some deeper problems and my family members could have received support from me. An answer could have been: "Carrots aren't your favorite, are they? I guess my problem is with broccoli. Anyway, we've got to see at night, so try to eat them. Your mom is a great cook, and even broccoli is—well, anyway, do you have any other problems or concerns?"

"Yeah, Dad, we do. What about . . ."

We all know somebody that we love to talk to, someone who just listens. Be to your children that kind of friend. Be the kind who, even though he has the right answer, knows that there is a right time and a wrong time for a right answer. A right answer at the wrong time can send a child to his room and can close a door that ought not to be closed. A right answer that closes a door can shut in trouble and shut out help.

If we will spend time with our children they will talk to us. If we listen with understanding, they will make decisions that will bring them down the right road. All of us—the educated, the rich, the poor, the executives, and the laborers—can do this. We can all listen. You and I can pray for this great ability, and through the priesthood we will receive it.

CHAPTER 7

FAMILY HOME EVENING AND FATHER

In my study of the effects on children of the family home evening program, one interesting and heartwarming discovery was the effect that conducting these family home evenings had on the father.

Several of the fathers involved felt nervous about conducting the meetings. They expressed feelings of inadequacy, saying such things as "I'm not a teacher; I never was and I never will be." I reassured them by explaining that many fathers have such feelings but are still able to have rewarding family home evenings. I promise them that if they would call the family together each week in a warm and relaxed atmosphere, the teaching part would not be the problem that they might imagine it to be.

One man didn't seem enthusiastic at all about my request that he and his family enter into the project of holding family home evenings each week for three months. He attempted to escape involvement by saying, with some embarrassment, "I can't teach." I assured him that if he would call the family together and do his best, the teaching part would work out all right; I think he only agreed because he lacked the courage to tell me he wouldn't do it.

As I left his house, he had little to say and I felt he wished that I had never called on him.

Three months later, I returned, by appointment, to call on him and his family. As I left my car and closed the door, his front door opened and he come out onto the well-lit porch to greet me. I've never met a friendlier man or experienced a warmer welcome.

He immediately called his family of five children together. He, his wife, and the children sat on a stone bench that ran from the fireplace to the other side of the room. I took a seat in front of them and after some conversation I asked him for a report. The children, ranging in age from teenagers to a five-year-old, burst in before he could respond and each one expressed enthusiasm for what had happened in the family home evenings.

Then the wife spoke. "It has been a wonderful experience for us," she said, and then with considerable emotion she added, "and the very best lessons we had were those Jerry taught."

I thought that Jerry was one of the children. I smiled and said, "That's quite a compliment for you, Jerry." I then asked, "Now, which one of you children is Jerry?"

The wife quickly replied, "Oh no, Jerry isn't one of the children; Jerry is my husband."

I was a bit embarrassed at my error and my eyes quickly focused on the father. He was looking down and for a time he remained silent. In a quiet and humble tone he spoke, "Aw, I didn't do so good."

His wife was forceful and sincere as she replied, "Jerry, when you taught us it just seemed so powerful. It just seemed as if we were a family. We'll never forget the things you said."

Jerry was deeply touched by these heartfelt words. He looked up and into my eyes and spoke, "I guess I did do pretty good." After a pause he said, "You know, I've always been kind of the black sheep of my family. Growing up, I felt that the others in the family were better than me. So I guess I sort of rebelled and didn't do much in the Church. I got so I just didn't even go."

I listened intently as he continued. "I didn't want to have these family home evenings because I knew they were part of the Church, and besides, I just didn't feel I could do it. But one night after my wife had taught a lesson one week and my daughter another week, I decided I'd try one."

His eyes grew moist as he said, "I'll never forget the feeling I had in my heart as I talked about good things with my family. It just seemed that I was for the first time the father that I was supposed to be. I felt so good about what I'd done that the next Sunday morning I decided to go over to the church. I've been going over there every Sunday since then and I've never been so happy in all my life."

We may not all be great teachers, but we are fathers. When ordinary fathers who hold the priesthood of God have the courage to "talk about good things" to our families, we at that moment become great teachers. Not that our grammar becomes perfect or that words flow from us like water from a well; rather, we simply unlock our hearts and let our families know what we hold dear.

If we as fathers will call our families together each week for family home evening, the Lord won't forsake us, and our supposed lack of skill as teachers will never be a problem. If your wife has considerable skill as a teacher (and many wives do) she can often lead the family discussion. But you should always be ready to say something like, "What your mom is saying reminds me of something that happened to me while I was in the army." Then go on and teach the kids heart to heart.

The children can also take turns giving all or part of the discussion. You don't have to teach every week. You will, of course, be the chief teacher some weeks, but your main duty is just to make sure that your family home evening is held on a night when you are always home. Then be certain to call the family together and preside. The father always presides. This means that you are in charge; it is your decision who will conduct and they, under your direction, will carry out the program.

Following are some helpful hints to assist you in carrying out the kind of family home evening that will bring instruction, inspiration, and joy to your family.

First, resolve and make a firm commitment not to become upset. Nothing can destroy a family home evening as quickly as when the father gets upset. This happens most often when the children don't behave exactly as the father feels they should. He gets frustrated, raises his voice, and . . .

Some years ago I felt a bit ornery one Monday evening. As we began our home evening, the children were poking at each other and acting wild. I became upset and announced in a loud voice, "Sit up straight and knock off the fooling around or else there is going to be some big trouble around here." The children could see by the red in my face that I was serious. They became quiet. I continued by saying, "I don't know why you can't sit still for a few minutes and listen. Now, I don't want to hear anything out of any of you until I finish this lesson. And when I finish I'm going to ask some questions. You'd better know the answers."

As the "discussion" progressed, my voice became louder, the children all sat up straight, and I had perfect discipline. Finally I finished the lecture and began to ask the questions. They knew every answer. I had taught the ideas very well. I then asked, "Do you children have any questions?"

My oldest son said in a subdued tone, "I do." He then asked, "Next week could Mom teach the lesson?"

His words and my feelings told me that in trying to do right, I had done wrong. I had taught ideas, but I hadn't taught my family. I had also driven the Lord's Spirit not only out of our house, but probably clear out of the neighborhood.

I have learned a few things since then. I still don't let the children get very far out of line—nor do they seem to want to—

but I've found better methods of discipline. I've determined to control myself, and, with the help of prayer, I've done it. I simply refuse to get upset during family home evening.

Another father tells me that if he feels that he is beginning to be upset at family home evening, he holds his hands in the shape of a "T" and calls time out, as athletes do in the heat of a contest. After calling time out he goes and gets a drink of water. He said, "I don't get upset anymore, but I do drink a lot of water."

Don't get upset at family home evening. And an even bigger order is not to get upset very often at all. Your family will be blessed indeed if you can be pleasant rather than surly. Some fathers feel that it's their role to be a hard sort of man. They speak sharply to their wives and children. Our families don't deserve such men. We avoid smoking and drinking, and that is as it should be, but some of us may feel that there is nothing wrong with being discourteous and unkind at home. It is possible, however, that a house filled with discourtesy and perhaps even with hatred is worse than one filled with smoke.

So be pleasant. Save your best and friendliest behavior for home. If you must be ornery, be ornery at work, where it matters less than it matters at home. Then go home and be pleasant. Just resolve to be pleasant at home—and especially during family home evening.

The second principle for fathers to follow in family home evening is to relax. This, of course, is closely related to staying pleasant. Remember that no one is looking in your window to see if you are doing everything just right. (If you are unsure of this, you can pull the shades.)

In our home, family home evening is not like the formal classes at the chapel. No law says we must sit in chairs; we often sit on the floor to make sure everyone feels relaxed. We don't follow a set procedure. Usually we talk for a while about whatever we want to talk about. We might then sing one or two or even five songs. Then, sometimes near the beginning of the evening, we all kneel down and have prayer.

Usually, as the father, I lead the family in a discussion from the manual, but sometimes we just talk. Other times the children lead the discussion or tell or read ideas and stories from the manual. I feel that once the family gets in a discussion there is no need to stop so that we can finish the lesson. Fathers get upset because they feel they must see that the lesson is taught and that the family members pay strict attention. That idea is partially correct, but when it becomes an obsession, family home evenings become unpleasant experiences.

A family home evening might be likened to a trip to Yellowstone Park. One way to visit this wonderful park would be: "Children, we are about to enter the park. Now, our goal is to see the park. So we'll need to hurry or we won't get through. As we travel we will see bears and rivers and elk and birds. But if you see these things, don't ask us to stop to look closely or we won't get through the park." In other words, you decide that seeing the park is the purpose of the trip. Then when you get home you can say, "We did it. We saw the park. We went all the way through."

That's not the way to see the park. A better way is to enter the park and see what you can see. You must stop along the way and see that day what you may never see again. You must let what you are doing sink completely in. Who cares if there will be some things that the park offers that will go unseen, at least on this trip? The important thing is to enjoy to its fullest what you do see. It's better to see one part of the park in a hundred relaxed ways than to strive to see a hundred parts of the park under the tension of haste.

Enter the home evening discussion with a relaxed attitude. "Let's see what we can see as we go along and when the time is gone, we'll eat apple pie and ice cream." Such an attitude allows a father to see his family as the true blessing they are. As the father is speaking, a small child might turn a somersault. Dad might be prompted to stop talking and say, "Look at that. Did you see what Marky did? Everyone move back and give him room. Why, I didn't know you could do that. You are getting to be a big boy. Don't all of you others think he's getting big?" By then Marky has been noticed and you say, "Okay, big boy, now you can sit down again because Daddy has a few more important things to say."

Another way to handle that would be to smack him on the rear as he goes over and tell him to sit still or he will get a few more swats. Either way works, but one way makes the child feel good, the father feel good, and the family feel good, and the other way makes everyone feel just the opposite. If you as a father are willing to relax during family home evening, and at other times, your family will enjoy home evenings. And they will also enjoy just plain being at home together.

We had an unusual family home evening one night. One of the children had brought a phonograph record of various college fight songs. We pulled the window drapes, put on the record, turned up the sound, and as a family we marched all around the house. We went upstairs, downstairs, and all over. Finally the record ended. Tired out by the fervent marching, we collapsed together and talked. It seems easier to talk about important things after an activity of this sort.

Another night we played a special game. One child hid himself and a second child found the first child and hid with him. The third child found the first two and hid with them. We continued until all ten of us were hiding together under a bed. That game really made us a close family.

After the game, we were all sitting on the floor. I asked Kathryn, who was about eleven years old, if she would like me to tell her about her future. She said she would. I began by saying, "All right, children, I want all of you to listen carefully while I tell Kathryn her future."

I had the family's complete attention as I spoke. "Kathryn, you are a beautiful girl. You will grow up and become a lovely young lady." Kathryn liked the story so far. I continued, "Someday, somewhere, either at school or at work or somewhere you will meet a young man and you will really like him and he will like you. After a time you will say, 'I love him.' Later, when he's been on a mission and you are ready, he will ask you to marry him. Then he will ask me if he can have you for his bride. I'll like him a lot and I'll agree.

"Then one day, very early in the morning I will come to your room and wake you up. I'll say, 'Kathryn, it's time to get up so that we can be on time.' We'll all get dressed and drive to downtown Salt Lake City. We'll park as close as we can to the temple. Then we will go inside. It is really special to go into the temple.

"Finally, we will be in a beautiful room in the temple. In the center of the room will be an altar. Around the altar will be soft cushions where you can kneel on one side and your husband-to-be can kneel on the other side.

"Your mother and I will be there, as will your dearest friends. A man of God will be there, a man who will have the power to seal things on earth and in heaven. This man will talk to you about your glorious life together with your chosen mate. Then he will have you and him kneel at the altar and hold hands. He will say the words that will unite you in marriage forever.

"Kathryn, that's what is going to happen to you. Won't that be something, when you go to the temple to be married? Just like when your mom and I went to the temple to be married. Married forever. Kids, won't it be something when each of you goes to the temple to be married?"

Then as the children looked on in rapt attention I said, "I love all of you so much. And I want to tell each one of you that this Church is true." I then said, "Now let's play some more games." They were ready.

I have learned that when you can relax with your family there will come those glorious moments when, in your own way, you can open your heart and share with your family the good things that are there. So, fathers, let's do it. Let's have family home evening in a relaxed, enjoyable way. By all means let's use the scriptures and other resources the Church provides, but most of all, let's use the resources of our hearts. And in those golden moments, perhaps one minute this week, five minutes next week, and so on, let us, as fathers, open our hearts and pour out the contents to our children. Such moments can and do make all the difference.

Chapter 8

TEACHING YOUR CHILDREN TO WORK

One summer day I was working for a farmer. The temperature was near 100 degrees and I was crawling slowly down a row of young onions, digging out weeds with a little knife. I must admit, I wasn't really having a wonderful time. The farmer drove by on his tractor, shouting to me to go a little faster. I tried to hurry, but I really wasn't very motivated. All I could think of was that I wished I was driving the tractor and he was digging the weeds.

The farmer wasn't my dad and he was paying me, so I don't blame him for wanting me to hustle. But I do think my feelings that day explain why some children are considered lazy—sometimes being lazy is the same as wanting to avoid torture. And weeding those onions in that sun was torture.

We fathers can teach our children to work and at the same time not torture them too much, if at all. Let's go back to the onion field. Assume that the farmer was my father; and further assume that he had no other help but me. Obviously I'd have to weed the onions—but it wouldn't have to be torture. All my father would have to do is say, "This morning you and I will weed the onions. I'll help you and we can have a few races. I think I can beat you. Then after lunch we'll go to town in the truck and get some tools. When we return we'll take the tractor and clean out that ditch over there."

Now, I don't know if safety would let me ride on the tractor with him or if I would be old enough to drive it. All I know is that if he'd do all he could as a father to treat me like an equal, even though the work would at times be hard, it would seldom if ever be torturous.

Fathers can and should get away from the "master and slave" concept and move toward a partnership program. And when we do, we can teach our children how to work.

I recall once when we had just purchased a new home. Our lack of finances demanded that we landscape it ourselves. Those who have undertaken such a task know what is involved before the grass becomes green, the scrubs take root, and the petunias paint their glorious pictures. It almost makes me tired just thinking about it.

There was much work to do. Rocks were everywhere. Our first task was to get rid of them. To me, that seemed like a perfect task for a boy. He could do that while I went to buy some sprinkler materials. I advised him of my plan. He seemed to have little enthusiasm. I told him to get busy and departed to the hardware store.

When I returned he had done very little. I scolded him and told him again to get busy. While I watched him, he worked fairly well, but when I turned away to do my work, he began to slow and finally he just sat there. When I saw his lack of effort I shouted at him. He seemed ready to cry and so I decided to try a different approach.

I needed a certain wrench, and I invited him to go to the store with me to get it. As we rode along, we talked about how the yard would look when we finished. At the store I asked him if he knew where the wrenches were. I let him lead the way. He found the wrench and I bought it.

When we arrived back home we talked about the rocks. I decided to work with him on moving them. While we worked, we talked. He seemed happy now doing work which had before seemed to bring him pain.

I had to get a few things done before dark. I told him I had to leave him but that I didn't think that in one half-hour he could clear an area of rocks. I drew a line around the area. I told him that if in one half-hour he could move all those rocks it would be a world's record. He said he could do it. I said, "I don't think you can."

He said, "Just watch."

I worked on my project and he on his. He did it. I inspected it and announced, "I can't believe it. Somebody helped you. Who was it?"

"Nobody," he replied. "I did it myself."

I called his mother out and told her of what he'd done. I told her, "We've got a worker for a son. I just don't know what I'd do without him."

Then we worked together on the project I was doing; he learned by watching and by handing me tools. Then I said, "Let's both see if by working together we can move all those rocks." He accepted the challenge and we did it.

As the days came and went we would often talk together about how beautiful the yard would look. We'd go together to get grass seed, scrubs, and other things. I'd ask his opinion about where certain plants should go. We were partners.

When the yard was beautiful I'd often remark that we had surely done a good job and that without him I couldn't have done it. And it was the truth.

I've noticed that my children hate to do the dishes. I believe that's because they don't like to be alone doing this chore. Now, I know they must do hard things and so I suppose they should do the dishes even if the task seems a bit difficult.

When one of our sons became old enough to do the dishes without breaking too many—his brothers and sisters also took turns—sometimes there were great arguments about who would do them. Sometimes when Mother would tell them to do the dishes she would then go into the other room to work. It really bothered this son to do the dishes all alone. He liked it when mother stayed there in the kitchen and helped him. It didn't seem like work then; it was pleasure. Mother made things seem easier. Sometimes when he and Mother did the dishes they even sang songs, and they played games like "twenty questions." It was fun to work like that. When the kitchen was cleaned up, Mother would say, "Look how our kitchen looks. It is the most beautiful kitchen in the world because it is clean and you helped to clean it."

When we moved from one town to another, my young son and I were taking a table from the home to the moving van. The table appeared too big to go through the door. I was puzzled about how to get it through and I asked the boy what he thought. He considered the matter and said, "If we turn it on its end and take these legs through first, then I think it will go."

I said, "Let's try it." We did as he had suggested and it worked. As we went toward the truck I looked at him and said, "You know, having you help is just like having a man."

He's always remembered that, and he says to me, "Remember when you told me that having me help was like having a man?"

We as fathers need to teach our children, even when they are young, that we respect their opinions. If we work with them, they won't appear lazy, but ambitious. If we will take the time to give them a vision of the end result, they will be willing to bring the vision about.

We don't have to live around a farm to teach our children to work. They can help us build partitions in the basement, plant gardens, clean rooms, work on cars, change tires, and paint walls. Sometimes we could do the work more quickly if they'd go and play and get out of our way, but then we all would be the losers.

They can paint even though it causes a little mess. They can saw, with supervision, on boards that don't need a perfect cut. They can hand you nails and bring tools. And they'll love it if while you work together, you talk and joke together. Children so raised will know how to do things and they'll want to do them.

A family had invited my family to a barbecue dinner. The father asked his teenage son to light the charcoal bricks in the broiler. The son lit a match but it went out before he got to the bricks. The father grabbed the matches and said, "Give me those. You can't do anything right." The father then lit the fire in the broiler and at the same time an unseen and destructively negative fire in his son's soul.

We need to be patient with our children. And some of our children require that we be more patient with them than with others. Some can do things quickly; others can't. Each must have time to succeed. If only that father who gave his son a "one match" chance to light the fire had been more patient. His son could have succeeded—on the second or maybe even the tenth match. And with success, he would have become more able to do the job with one match the next time.

It is easy for fathers with great talents to do things themselves while their children watch. (For some others of us, it's easier to let our children do things because we really aren't as good at it as they are.) But if you really are mechanical or handy, force yourself to let your children perform. Give them time; give them all the chances they need. Restrain yourself from taking over and someday they'll be as good or better at it than you are. When they hit a snag in the task, let them think about it. Make certain they have every chance to work it out themselves before you step in. And try to step in on their invitation rather than on your impatient promptings.

A young son of mine in a temper tantrum had torn down a bulletin board in his room. I was upset that he had done this destructive thing. I took him to his room. I sat in a chair and told him to put the bulletin board back up. I told him that that would teach him not to destroy anything. I knew he couldn't get it back up and that after some time he'd learn his lesson.

He began to work. He could hardly lift the bulletin board, let alone hold it in place to put the nails in the proper holes. He struggled and struggled. He knew I was upset and he felt he must succeed. I sat watching. I was pleased that he could see how difficult it was. Then to my amazement I saw that the little guy had almost succeeded. But then just as one tap with the hammer would bring success, the whole thing fell down. I felt sorry for him.

But he didn't give up. Back to the task he went. I wasn't nearly as upset now. I wanted to get up and help, but I decided to watch. Again he almost had it. I had to restrain myself from helping. He held it in place and slowly reached for the hammer. He tapped one nail in and then another. He had done it. I couldn't believe it. I had not thought it possible.

We sat on the bed and I praised his talent. We then talked about the misery that comes when we wreck things and about the joy that comes as we build. This rather negative story ended positively. It taught me that our children have unusual abilities to work and to accomplish if we will let them try.

Part of work is making decisions about what is to be done. My son, at the end of one baseball season, had to return a little league uniform to the team manager. He had the uniform and we got into the car. I started the engine but didn't put it in gear. After a few seconds he said, "Let's go."

I asked, "Where?"

He said, "To the manager's."

I said, "Where's that?"

He said, "I don't know."

I said, "Neither do I. I've not lived here any longer than you have and I don't know where your manager lives."

He said, "It would be in the phone book." I didn't answer. After a few seconds he jumped from the car and got the phone book and returned and handed it to me. I handed it back to him. He started turning pages, put his finger under the coach's name and showed me. I didn't reply. He read the address and closed the book. I didn't move the car. He said, "Let's go."

I asked, "Where?"

He called out the address. I started forward but didn't turn at the corner. He said, "Hey, turn here." I then turned but went beyond the next turn. Soon he knew he must direct my every turn. We made it and delivered the uniform. He felt he had a dumb dad. But now he knew how to find where people lived in a big city. It's easy to do things for our children and we often do that. But once in a while—the more the better—we need to let them figure it out themselves. They can, you know; and when they do, they grow.

Chapter 9

BE A LITTLE FUNNY AT TIMES

What a blessing it is to a family when the father can act a bit goofy once in a while. Some of us are serious almost all the time. We are funny at parties with our friends and we goof off there, but with our children we act as if a little fun and games would suddenly end the world.

We all know that life is serious business and we can't just laugh it off. But there is so much of life that can be laughed off. If we do it, we will have the power to endure the serious and the sometimes sad experiences.

Once I gave some of my children a ride to school. I was in a particularly jolly mood and made many remarks that the children felt were funny. I even sang a little for them. (They also thought this was funny, although I hadn't intended it to be.) We had a ball as we rode along.

Later, one of my children reported that another child had said to him, "Your dad is crazy." Then, after a pause, he had continued, "I sure wish my dad was crazy."

King Benjamin in the Book of Mormon was inspired by the Lord to tell his people not to allow their children to fight and quarrel one with another. Now, that is a big order. One way to keep your children from being contentious is to forbid contention.

If they fight or argue, send them to the other room or punish them. In other words, every time they fight and quarrel you can, because you are bigger and have authority, make them submit to more peaceful behavior. But sometimes the contention caused in putting down contention is more contentious than the original contention. And that, as you can see in the previous sentence, is a lot of contention.

I feel that there is a better way. If a father will joke with the children and be pleasant he can set an atmosphere that stifles contention. At dinnertime it is not uncommon for problems to arise. Someone might say, "Please pass the gravy." When it isn't passed, he almost shouts, "Pass the gravy!"

The mother says, "Don't shout."

The person then says, "I've asked five times and he can't hear."

Someone else says, "He never can hear anything."

And there is contention.

To settle it, the father can say, "Everyone be quiet. I don't want to hear any talk. Just everybody shut up." And somehow about that time the food isn't quite as delicious as it had been. But at least contention is gone—or is it?

But if at dinner the atmosphere is somewhat like it is when a group of friends are having a picnic, then little contention arises. Father can make dinner a picnic. He does it by being cheerful, by telling a few crazy jokes, and by speaking of interesting and inspiring observations, by being positive.

I like to start dinner by saying, "Well, here we are, the greatest family on earth. And tonight we see before us some delicious steak that has been ground into hamburger and has been mixed with this choice macaroni." The children usually smile, and I continue, "Tonight our prayer at the table will be given by one of the greatest people I know, a person who is a blessing to all of us, a person we all love, a good-looking, intelligent, wonderful person."

By now each of the children says, "But, Dad, I said it last night." Then I call on one to pray. The family is in a good mood. If Father praises the food, and thus the mother, she beams, and the whole family has a delicious, uncontentious meal.

A funny father can help the children start the day right by waking up the family with good humor. You could pinch a daughter's toe and say, "Marinda, you beautiful angel, it is time to arise. Allow the world to see your radiant beauty. Count to ten, Marinda, so that I'll know you are awake. Get up, because there are only three hundred days until Christmas. Come on, it's time to get up, my beautiful princess." Now, that's a good way for a girl to start the day.

Some people don't like nicknames. But I'm afraid I do. I like to call my children nicknames. When I served in the military in Korea, I learned the word *skoshie*, which means "little." When I got home and had a little son I couldn't help but call him "Skoshie." Our little daughter Marinda was our new child once and we called her "Newy."

We call our boy Dwight, "Crow." He got that name in an interesting way. I used to work in the Church's Indian program. The name Dwight rhymes with the word white. Wishing to give him an Indian name, I called him "White Cloud." Once a huge Crow Indian came to stay at our house during general conference. I was proud to introduce my son to this giant man of the Crow tribe. I said, "And this is my son, White Cloud."

He said in a deep voice, "What you call him?"

I repeated, "White Cloud."

He said then with some sternness, "From now on, don't call him 'White Cloud.' From now on call him 'White Crow.'"

Of course I didn't want any trouble with the Indians, so I called him "White Crow." And to this day I still call him "White Crow" or just plain "Crow."

Whether it is nicknames or funny remarks, your special brand of humor can brighten your home and chase away contention. Your family needs a continual priesthood blessing. Not one that comes from the laying on of hands, but one that happens just because you came home—a blessing of a father who is happy, who sees the funny side of life, who can solve problems with wit as well as with wisdom.

This is a difficult thing for some fathers to do. To some, they and humor just don't mix. But, fathers, we can improve in being good natured; and when we do, we set the family mood meter at the highest level of happiness. If you can't do anything else that is funny, you can at least sing. In many cases that might be the beginning of humor—if not the end.

Chapter 10

PRAY FOR YOUR FAMILY AND FOR YOURSELF

When we lived in Kentucky, my son played junior varsity basketball. Most of the crowd at one game were Baptists, and they were almost all cheering for my son's opponents. The game ended in a tie. The first overtime also ended in a tie. By this time most of the fans were in a bit of a frenzy. The second overtime came down to its final agonizing seconds and still the score was tied. With just two seconds to go, my son got the ball and shot. The shot missed, but the whistle blew—he had been fouled.

As he went to the foul line to shoot the deciding shot the opposing coach called time out. In the few seconds of the time out I had time to pull myself together and to do some nearly logical thinking. I decided to pray, and then I thought, "But the Lord doesn't care whether or not he makes it, nor does he care who wins. Besides," I thought, "all the Baptists in here are praying that he'll miss, and it's hard to out-pray a Baptist."

So I decided I wouldn't pray about it. The whistle blew and the boys took their places for the foul shot. My son stepped to the foul line. My heart pounded. As the referee handed him the ball, I lost control of my rational reasoning and found myself silently begging the Lord, "Please let him make it! Please!" Sometimes we get to the point that we don't know what else to do but pray.

The shot went up and in. The other team quickly took the ball and threw it in bounds, but the game was over. I came down out of the stands and hugged my son. He didn't even seem embarrassed.

I'm still quite sure that in most cases the Lord doesn't care who wins a ball game. He knows that we learn lessons in both victory and defeat. But I do know that he does care about many things—he cares very much.

He cares when our children are walking in crooked and dark paths that will lead them to misery rather than joy. He cares when they are hurting inside as they long to find their place in a difficult world. He cares when our children seem to turn away from our counsel and listen to other voices that would cause them to forsake the truth and choose a lie as a lifestyle. He cares when we sit in the late night and early morning hours wanting to know why our children are not yet home.

Fathers, the Lord cares as much or more about our children than we do. Any matter that we desire to discuss with him in prayer, and that involves the spiritual or physical well-being of our children, is important enough to discuss with the Lord. I am convinced that someday we will discover that one of the most powerful influences we have wielded in raising our children was the yearning, pleading prayers that we uttered for the welfare of our children. Such prayers, spoken by the power of the priesthood and in the name of Jesus Christ, in behalf of our families, are always heard in the royal courts on high.

Not all the shots our children shoot in the game of life will go in the basket. But with our prayers and our love and support they'll score often enough to keep trying, and they'll win.

As often as possible, when you know you are alone, kneel down and talk to the Lord about each of your children. Talk to the Lord as you would to a friend. Mention each child by name.

Give the Lord a complete report on the present status of the child. Something such as: "Heavenly Father, as thou knowest, my sixteen-year-old daughter, Susan, is having a difficult time. We just moved here and she is heartbroken because all of her friends are back in the place we just left. She's come to me and we've talked and she's cried to me. But Heavenly Father, there is little I can do. Therefore, I come to thee. Please help her. Please cause some things to happen at the school that will prompt some of the girls there to open their closed friendship circle just enough to let her in. Please let her find at school a friend as dear as those she left behind."

We as fathers pray and then do all we can. Then there's nothing else we can do except pray more and do more. And through our prayers for our children miracles can and do occur.

Our mightiest and most helpful prayers for our children's good might well be prayers that we offer in behalf of ourselves, prayers such as: "Heavenly Father, my son and I just don't seem to communicate. Somehow whenever we talk I get upset and become unreasonable. Then I say things that make matters worse. Please give me the power to listen to him and to understand him. I know that although I try desperately to help him, I'm often really not a solution to his problem, but rather a cause. Help me to be more patient with him. Give me understanding. Direct my relationship with him. Please help me to have the power to help him."

As we pray, the Lord can and will help us. He will cause our priesthood power to swell within our breasts and make us equal to the mightiest of all tasks—that of being a father.

When the family hour was changed to the family home evening program and before Monday evenings had been designated as the usual night for such family gatherings, I had an experience I'll long remember.

It was summer and our sacrament meeting ended early, so we

decided that we'd hold our home evening after the services. The children were told before we departed for church that right after we got home we'd go to the back lawn for family home evening.

As we arrived home, some of the neighborhood children were playing nearby. They had a huge cardboard barrel that one of them would sit in and ride head over heels while the others rolled the barrel. It looked like great fun, even to an old father like me, and I'm sure its enticement for a small boy was unusually strong. But nonetheless we had little difficulty getting the children to gather with us on the back lawn. After the opening portion of our family gathering, and just as I was beginning to tell a story, our five-year-old son, Devin, announced that he had to go in the house. His reason was one with which I could not argue, so he was excused to go.

We awaited his return, but he didn't come back. We carried on for a while but then closed the activity a bit early. I went past the front of the house and out near the street. I pulled him out of the cardboard barrel. I was a patient, kind, wonderful father as I calmly said, "Come in the house with me."

He had a hostile tone in his voice as he announced, "I want to stay here. You never let me play."

I was no longer quite so calm. I raised my voice and stated, "That's about all you do is play." He replied and I replied and we headed toward the house. He came willingly because he had to; I was holding his hand. I walked faster than he could walk but he kept up because I was dragging him.

We went down the hall toward the room where he slept. I opened the door, pulled him ahead of me into the room, hit him hard enough on the rear to hurt his feelings, and as I closed the door I raised my voice above his screams and said, "If you can't stay at family home evening, maybe you can stay in your room." As I slammed the door I said, "Now you stay in there and don't you come out."

There we were: I was sitting in a chair on one side of a door and he was kicking and screaming on his bed on the other side of the door. As I sat there I began to calm down. I wondered why I couldn't handle such a matter without getting so upset. As I looked at the closed door that separated my son and me, I started to pray. "Why does it have to be this way? Why do doors that ought to be open sometimes get closed? Why can't my son and I understand each other?"

As I sat in my chair looking at the closed door I wanted so much for it to open. And I began to hope that this little boy that I loved so dearly would forget my words and come through the door to me.

Soon my wish was granted. The door flew open and out he came. In a rebellious tone, he announced, "I'm coming out!"

I quickly jumped up, pulled him back into his room, and said, "I told you to stay in there."

The door had been opened, but not the right way. And now it seemed closed tighter than ever. Again we were separated by the door. Again I searched within. Time passed, and my heart was filled with an overwhelming love for this boy, my son. Again, I prayed for the door to open. I considered opening it. But I knew I must open it right or else it could teach what I didn't want to teach.

By now the little son had ceased his cries and his room was silent. After a time, the door opened just a crack, and then a little wider. Finally it was opened just wide enough that I could see him. He was crying again. Only this time he was crying in a different way. This time his tears were not those of rebellion but rather they were the tears of the heartbroken. As I looked into his eyes and he into mine, he spoke with softness, "Daddy, I'm sorry."

My reply was quick and sincere. "My son, I am, too." I then beckoned him with my hand and said, "Come here." He came over and stood by my side as I sat in the chair. I put my arm around his shoulder and pulled him close. How good it felt to have him with me again! I told him, "Devin, did you know that when you left us tonight we didn't have a family home evening? When you left, we didn't have a family because you were gone."

I talked to my son. The Spirit of the Lord was there. What a joy it is to talk to your son when the Spirit of the Lord is there! I told him of my love for him, of my pride in him. I told him that because he was so easy to like, everyone admired him. I told him of the great good he could do if he'd just be where he ought to be and do what he ought to do. I talked to him about his future and even about the time when he would serve a mission. Because of the Spirit that was there he seemed to understand all that I said.

Then I realized that he was just a little boy and that I'd talked to him a long time. I decided I should let him go. I hugged him one last time, whirled him around, and hit him again on the rear (the blow was as hard as before, only this time it didn't hurt), and said, "Now you go and play."

He crossed the room to leave. But just as he was about to disappear down the hall, he stopped. He turned around and looked back at me and said, "Dad, I don't want to go and play. I want to stay here with you."

I called him back. This time I took him on my lap and held him as close as I could. We sat in silence and rocked back and forth. The Lord's quiet warm influence bound us together as a father and son and we were as one.

Oh, may the Lord bless us as fathers that when things go wrong, as they sometimes do, and when doors close between a father and a child we'll call upon him who is the Father of us all to open the door for us or to help us know how to open it. He'll give us the priesthood power to open the door and keep it open. If we'll do all we can, he will magnify us as fathers and he'll bless us with the love, understanding, discipline, and all else we need in order to be a blessing in every way to our children.

Chapter 11

SHOW AND TELL YOUR LOVE TO YOUR FAMILY

Because of the way some of us were raised it seems very difficult for us to say the words "I love you." Mothers seem to say it with greater ease, but some fathers just can't quite ever get the words out. That doesn't mean that we don't feel it—it's just that saying it is difficult.

Some fathers don't have any trouble showing affection and saying gentle and loving things to family members. But many fathers can't help but appear a little hard on the outside; they feel that a man's role is to be a little rough, a little stern, and not sentimental.

Stern fathers offer a certain kind of firm stability to the family. But they need to add just a slightly new, more loving dimension to their natures.

It just isn't right for your children to have to guess whether or not you love them. They'll always suspect that you do, but once in a while why not come right out and tell them? You can do it. It might make you nervous, but you can do it.

My own father had a hard time saying "I love you." As a

matter of fact, I do not recall that I ever heard him say that to anyone. He was good to me and because of all that he did for me I was very suspicious that he loved me; I really knew he did, but he never would say it.

He had been a miner in the silver mines and later he became a poultryman. He was a rough outdoorsman and had expertise in hunting and fishing. He was really a man's man and to me he was a great father. But he never said, "George, I love you." One day he did come close to telling me he loved me.

I was about to depart on my mission to England. I was nearly twenty-two years old. (They didn't go at age nineteen then.) It was in the middle of November and there was snow on the ground. I was to depart in three days. Since I was the youngest of nine children, when I departed all the children would be gone from home. My father must have felt a bit saddened by this. He and I were alone in our big kitchen where we seemed to live our lives (seldom did we go in the front room). He stood looking out the window that was the upper portion of our back door. He suddenly said, "George, come over here." I went to his side and looked out. About a hundred yards beyond our barn was a thicket of brush and trees. There in the snow on the edge of the brush was a beautiful Chinese pheasant. My father spoke again, "George, get the gun."

I replied, "Dad, the season ended over a week ago."

I'll never forget what he said next because it was the most loving thing he ever spoke to me. He said, "I know that. You go get the gun and go out there and shoot that pheasant. And while you're doing it, I'll call the cops and they'll come and arrest you and you won't have to go."

I was by this time much taller than he. I looked down at him and he looked away. I put my hand on his shoulder and then pulled him close to me. Together we cried. My dad, my dear dad, had for the first time said in the best words he could muster, and in the best way he knew how, what I had longed to hear for twenty-two years. He had said, "George, my son, I love you."

It means so much to our children to hear "I love you" from their dads. They don't need to hear it every minute, but they ought to hear it a little more often than once every twenty-two years. We can say "I love you" in a number of ways. When Dwight was six years old, I took him from Salt Lake City to Provo one day. While I worked at BYU he played with friends in the neighborhood where we had once lived. At the day's end I picked him up and we drove toward home. We stopped for a snack; we took our order from the cafe and walked about twenty-five yards to the bank of the Provo River. There, sitting on a log, we ate. I looked at the river and then at Crow on the opposite end of the log.

I spoke, "I've got a better hamburger than you."

He answered, "Mine's just like yours."

I added, "My milkshake is better than yours."

He replied, "Mine's the same flavor as yours."

"My fries are better," I said.

"I've got ones just like yours," he replied convincingly.

After a pause I looked at him and said, "I've got one thing that you haven't got."

He was certain that I didn't have and asked with a challenge, "What?"

"I've got a son that I call Crow. And I'm sitting on a log with him and I love him with all my heart. And you don't have that."

Crow didn't answer. He just looked at me for a few seconds, then bit into his hamburger and with his other hand threw a rock in the river. I had bested him and he knew it.

I've also found that when I lead in family prayer I can express my love for my family. It's a little easier when your eyes are closed and theirs are too. Blessings and ordinations are also a splendid time for a father to express deep feelings of love for the child his hands are touching. Letters and notes are an excellent way for both the timid and the bold to express love. A note or letter can be read, reread, and saved forever.

Of course, saying "I love you" can be but a hollow phrase if we don't surround it by deeds that prove our love. But most of us do the deeds. My father surely did. Nonetheless, just because we perform deeds of love is no reason not to express words of love. Then our children are twice blessed, and that's what every child needs.

So pray for, look for, and be ready for those natural, wonderful times when you look at a child and your heart says, "I'm a fortunate man to have him or her as a child. Oh, how proud I am and how my heart is filled with love." Then open your mouth and let your heart speak. Your words of pure love will be a priesthood blessing of the highest order.

Chapter 12

LOVE THEIR MOTHER

I searched as a young man for a woman who deserved the very best. When I found her I asked her to marry me. And of course, she quickly agreed. Now, before you throw me out and refuse to read the last few pages of the book, let me explain this bold assertion. I didn't say that I was the best. All I said was that I found a girl who deserved the best. And I still say that. She does deserve the best, as does your sweetheart and wife.

To give a wife the best, as you probably have discovered, you don't have to be handsome. And you don't have to be rich. All you have to do is to be good and, as Merlin told King Arthur, "love her, love her, love her."

Your whole purpose in life should be to give your wife the best. That means to give her the very best you that is possible. As you live honorably and faithfully, you will bring her great joy. The two of you will, as the years go by, fall ever more in love. And as you love her, she will return that love in full and more.

From the love of the two of you, your children will be blessed with the best. They will see "beauty all around" because they will know "love at home." As fathers, we are universal in acclaiming the fact that our children deserve the best, and love at home is indeed the best gift, the best memory, and the best inheritance a child can receive.

It appears that the most important element in raising happy, well-adjusted children is for children to perceive that their parents love each other. A husband and wife who are as one because of a deep love make successful parents. They may not understand all that child psychology teaches, but they succeed anyway.

Such parents can be very strict with their children and it seems to bring good results. Or they can be a bit less strict and that will also work. Others, who do not enjoy a deep love as parents, find little success no matter what they try.

The best thing, then, that a father can do for his children is to love their mother. Such things cannot be hidden. Nor can a lack of love go undetected by the child, who sees with his heart. Along with the undercurrents of love that can be felt by your children, you should also say aloud to your wife, in the presence of your children, "I love you."

Once at a family home evening we were all saying good things about each other. Finally, Mother became the target of such remarks. Each child said what he appreciated about her. My oldest son, Matt, said, "Dad, if I said all the good things I know about Mom, we would be here all night."

I picked up the cue from there. The stage had been set and I came on with the power of someone who speaks at exactly the right time. I said, "Children, I feel just like Matt and the rest of you do. I love your mother with all my heart. She makes my life one of complete happiness. She is a perfect wife."

Marilyn beamed as she listened. The next week we had some of the most delicious meals that you can imagine. Yes, indeed, "there is beauty all around when there's love at home."

In the everyday experiences of each of us, there come perfect opportunities to say to our wives with words, cards, or flowers, "I love you." Such a message will make your wife glow with joy and will cause your children to feel the security of something special in their hearts.

This poem (whose authorship I have not been able to establish) describes one way of expressing your love at a dinner table:

> She looked at him.
> Her heart was all a flutter.
> He had just written
> "I love you" in the butter.

There are many ways to express love, and many motivations. At a Church meeting, discussing the role of the husband, the speaker told of the joy that comes when a husband sends flowers to his wife. He spoke so convincingly that one of his listeners went to the florist right after the session, sent a dozen roses to his wife, and charged them to the speaker.

No matter who we charge it to, we get the full value out of every act of love that tells both our wife and our children that we are in love.

When we speak words of love to our mates, the children are not usually there to hear, but they feel the results. Love unites a husband and wife, and makes them as one. Children are not confused when the mother's voice and direction and the father's voice and direction are as one voice.

I was once driving down a Salt Lake City freeway, going with Marilyn to a meeting in Rose Park. There are two exits from the freeway that are very close together. One leads to Rose Park and the other leads back toward the city. As we approached these exits, I felt inspired to tell Marilyn that I loved her. I spoke the words, "I love you," and became so excited by what I'd said that I took the wrong exit.

We were headed away from rather than toward Rose Park. I announced, "We are on the wrong road." But then I was inspired again as I said, "No, we aren't on the wrong road. As long as we are together and in love and living righteously we can't be on the wrong road." We turned around anyway.

When it comes to teaching our children, we are not on the wrong road if we as husbands would rather die than bring heartache to the girl of our dreams—our chosen mate for all eternity. We are not on the wrong road if we can say, with conviction, "My wife deserves the best and I'm going to give her the best—my total love."

To give her your love, give her the privilege of living with a man who honors his priesthood with all his heart; a man who is honest in all his dealings; a man who shuns filth in its every form, be it a dirty joke, a vulgar word, or a lustful look; a man who prays privately, with his family, and especially with her; a man who serves his fellowmen, knowing that as King Benjamin said, "when ye are in the service of your fellow beings ye are only in the service of your God." (Mosiah 2:17)

Give her a man who earns an honorable living; a man who loves to come home and who saves his most pleasant words, smiles, and actions for his family; a man whose first priority is his family; a man who loves his wife, loves her, loves her.

In concluding this book, let me share with you an experience that has given me great direction in my role as father.

Some years ago I was serving as a bishop. At the same time I was working on a doctor's degree at a university and holding a full time job. My children felt I was spending too much time away from them. I was under some strain, fearing that because of my desire to succeed in so many areas I was really failing as a man.

One Sunday evening all the members of my ward had gone home. I had stayed on for a while to complete some work. I walked into the chapel to turn off the lights before departing for home. I felt lonely in the empty chapel. As I stood there I felt that my back would not bear for another day the heavy burdens which I was carrying.

I fell to my knees near the pulpit and cried to the Lord. I told him, as one friend would another, my deepest concerns. I poured out the feelings of my soul to him and described in detail my seemingly insurmountable tasks. When I finished, I remained kneeling. And as I did I heard him speak to me in my heart. The answer he gave me was all I needed, for he said just three things:

Go forward.
Do your best.
Love your family.

I arose a new man. My burdens had been made light. I'd keep going. I would spend less time on the unimportant things in the ward, and I might not get "A" grades in school, but I'd keep going. I'd do my best, and that would be success. And most of all, I'd love my family. Oh, how I'd love them! I'd love my wife and I'd tell her so. I'd spend time with my children, and I'd know that such is the highest form of Church work.

And so I say to you, to all who, with me, are honored with the calling of a father, let us:

Go forward.
Do our best.
And love our families.

The Winner is Father

News: . . . the Transit Authority announced that, if the okay is given to proceed with the project, it will require four years for completion. That's the news. And now back to the Marve Levy Show.

Marve: Hello, and welcome back. This is the Marve Levy Show. If you were listening during the last hour you heard our guest Nolan Simmons outline his views on the increased role personal computers will have in the education of our children. Fascinating man—maybe we can get him back again.

This last half-hour will be open line. I'm sure you don't want to hear another of my tirades on the world's ills, so call in and you can go on your own personal gripes . . . Richard, you're on the air.

Caller: Hello, Marve. Am I on?

Marve: You sure are. What's troubling you?

Caller: Marve, I don't have anything to complain about, but I sure enjoy your show. That last guy was great! Anyway, I work in my little wood shop in the evenings and I'm a regular listener of yours. I've heard you enough to know you hate sentimental stuff. So I'm a little hesitant to call, because I don't have any great thing to say or profound question to ask. But Marve, don't cut me off. I'll only take a minute. I just had to call and announce that two hours ago my wife gave birth to a six-pound, four-ounce baby girl. And that has made me the happiest man in the world. I'll hang up now so you can get on with your other calls.

Marve: Oh, good. Just what the world needs—a "Happiest Man." I'll tell you what the world needs. It needs more guys who know that if we don't get on the ball, nobody will be happy at all. Old Richard needs to quit smelling the roses and start pulling some weeds. I can't believe it. Fifty thousand watts being used to announce the birth of a baby! It's no wonder this country is in such bad shape. We've got a bunch of know-nothing people out there who can't see the big issues because they are too busy bragging about having a baby. We'll see how happy that guy feels as he watches that baby grow up in a world as corrupt as this one . . . Yeah, go ahead, you're on the air. What's on your mind? Probably how to get your cat to eat the new calorie-free cat food. What is the world coming to? Go ahead.

Caller: Hey, Marve, lighten up. I've never heard you so ornery. You must have sat down on the wrong side of your microphone. Give the guy a break. Maybe what this country needs is more guys who feel they are the world's happiest men. Marve, quit being so cynical. Just relax and listen to what I've got to say and don't get upset. I just wanted to congratulate Richard on his new little girl. But I feel like I'm seven times happier than him because my wife and I have seven beautiful children.

Marve: Seven! Haven't you ever heard of family planning!"

Caller: We sure have, and we're still planning—to have two or three more.

Marve: That's disgusting. And just who's doing the planning? You? I'll bet your wife isn't.

Caller: Oh, yeah. We plan together. She always wanted a big family. She loves being a mother, and there's nothing in the world that is as much fun as being a father. You know that, Marve. I've heard you mention your two daughters, so you know what it is. Hey, I've gotta go, but I challenge old Richard who just called in. I'll bet I'm happier than he is.

Marve: Okay. If you say so . . . I'm glad he hung up before I had to cut him off. I give up. Ignorance is bliss. What's the use? I try to talk sense, but maybe tonight we'll just turn the phone lines over to the village dumbbells who want to talk about "happiness." . . . Jim, you're on the air. Don't tell me you're happier than our last caller because you have twelve kids. Man, I can't believe it! Two's enough for me. I love 'em, but I just wish . . . Oh, well, I guess being a family man isn't my thing. But anyway . . . so you've got twelve.

Caller: No. We don't have twelve. We just have one. But it took us twelve years to get that one. The first year we were married it broke our hearts when we found out we couldn't have a baby. We kept praying and hoping, but it just didn't happen. Then just a year ago we adopted a little boy, and I'm holding him on my lap now. He's grabbing at the phone. I wish you could see him, Marve. Today the final papers were signed. I just didn't know until we got this little guy how I could ever love anyone so much more than I love myself. I'm glad Richard is now a father, but there is no way he could be as happy as I am. Even that guy with seven can't be as happy as me. When it comes to happiness, I'm the champ.

Marve: Ah, well! We're on a roll. Let's just go ahead and waste the entire half-hour. Okay, so this guy thinks he beats out everybody so far. Let's limit our calls to men. You gals leave the calling to the men. Then later, when we need some people who understand big problems, we'll let you ladies take over the show . . . Hello. You're on the air.

Caller: Marve, I've been listening, and I love what I'm hearing. I've never called in before, but tonight I can't hold back. I don't think these other guys know what real happiness is. I'm the father of three. My former wife has them living with her. I know that doesn't sound like a happy story—as a matter of fact, it has completely broken my heart. When Judy and I married we dreamed we'd be the happiest couple who ever lived. But it just didn't work out. I don't know exactly what happened, but everything fell apart. There was a lot of bitterness. But today, when I took the children back after having them for the weekend, Judy met me at the front door and we stood there and talked. She seemed to have a different spirit about her. She told me that the children like being with me and that they love and respect me. I've never heard anything that meant more to me than hearing that. Just before I turned to go, each of the two smallest ones hugged me and said, "Thank you, Daddy. I love you." Then there's Nick, our fourteen-year-old—he has resented me since the divorce, and that hurts. But as I was about to go, he asked, "Can you come to my game Thursday?" Before I could answer, Judy quickly said, "He told me he always tries harder when his dad is there." I looked into his eyes and choked out the words, "Sure, son, I'll be there. I'll always be there." He smiled, and something deeply meaningful went between us. My tears were flowing as I turned to go. Then Judy said, "Thanks, Sid, for being such a good dad." Excuse me, Marve. I can hardly talk here . . . but anyway, that sure did make me happy—maybe even the happiest man in the world.

Marve: Hmm! That one hit me hard. I knew what he meant when he said that somehow everything fell apart. I just hope that I . . . well, that I can keep being there for my girls. But that's personal, and I'm not gonna uncover my heart. The rest of you can go on expressing your feelings, but I've found you can't trust feelings, so count me out. That's what Sarah has done. Anyway, when it comes to happiness, well, I'm a long ways from being a winner. Maybe our next caller will be our winner.

Caller: Marve, I sense a real human streak coming out of your supposedly hard shell. But as you continue to air applications for the happiest man, I feel I'm your winner. A lot of people would disagree, and at times I would, too. But right now, this very moment, I feel I'm indeed the world's happiest man. You see, I'm married to my childhood sweetheart. During my life, I have had a history of having all my dreams come true. Just about everything I've ever wanted, I've got. Even this year's Super Bowl winner was my team.

Marve: Well, no wonder you're so happy! My team didn't even make the play-offs. We'll put you down as a potential winner. Thanks for bringing up sports. Sports, I understand—it's family life that baffles me. Thanks for the call.

Caller: No, no, I'm not finished. I didn't call to discuss sports. Charleen and I have three teenage children. All of them are ideal kids. I'm a supervisor at work and have had several promotions. But two months ago, while I was playing basketball during my lunch hour, I suddenly felt exhausted. The next day I didn't have the energy to get out of bed. Charleen drove me to the doctor. One exam led to another. I hoped for the best, but I got the worst—I've been diagnosed as having bone cancer. They have filled in for me at work, and things are going fine there. My overriding concern has been the family. Charleen has been brave, but at times I hear her crying in the night. The children couldn't seem to bear the news when I told them. They never want to discuss the subject. They try to act cheerful, but there is gloom in their eyes. They've never wanted much in the way of fancy clothes and that, even though we've given them good things. I think all they've really wanted from me was for me to just be a good dad.

But the reason I called isn't to burden you with these things. I wanted to call because just an hour ago the three children came to where Charleen and I were sitting in the front room. They said they wanted to talk. The oldest, Kevin, had been appointed spokesman. As best I recall, he said, "Dad, we, uh . . . we've been, uh, thinking, and, uh . . ." His voice broke, and for a second or two he was silent. But then he took a deep breath and continued. "Dad, we need you. We've done some praying, and we feel you won't die."

The others nodded their agreement, and Kevin continued. "But we don't know what will happen. So we, uh, well, we want you to know something. You see, Dad . . ." Kevin then began to sob, as did the other two and Charleen. Finally, he continued. "You see, well, it's just that you're the best father who ever lived. And whether you stay here with us or die, we promise you that we'll live our lives in a way that will make you the proudest man who ever lived."

None of us could say more. Charleen and I stood up by the three kids. I held Kevin in my arms and never wanted to let go—then Clark, and then thirteen-year-old Laura. Then I held my sweetheart. Finally, all five of us were in one big embrace.

Marve, as we stood there as one family, for just a few minutes there I knew what heaven is like. And knowing that makes me feel that I'm your luckiest, most blessed, and happiest man.

(Silence filled both phones. Then the caller spoke softly.)

That's it, Marve. And Marve, I sense that things aren't so good for you and Sarah. Hold on to her, Marve. Hold on to her. And to all you other guys out there, take real good care of your wife and those . . . those . . . uh . . . those wonderful children. See you later, Marve.

Marve: Hmm! I feel like I should sign off and go home. At least I wish I could go home. But . . . Who's next? . . . You're on the air.

Caller: Marve, I don't know if I can pull myself together after that. I agree, that guy's the champ. But I had a good few minutes today, myself. My wife had to go out tonight and I was home alone. At least I would have been home alone if it hadn't been for our three-year-old and the seven-month-old twins. I can manage the fast food place where I work, but, man, getting the kids fed and bathed and in bed—that takes more than an MBA! But I did it! Then I cleaned up the kitchen and vacuumed. I mean, things were standing tall when Maggie came home. When she walked in the front room and heard the quiet and saw the order, you should have seen the look on her face. I'm learning my father did most things better than I do, but I'm a better house-husband than he is. And the way Maggie looked at me and hugged me tonight makes me feel that I'm at least the minor league happiest man in the world.

Marve: Well, a happy house-husband. Maybe I should have been a bit more helpful. But too late now . . . Hello. You're on the air.

Caller: Good show, Marve! I didn't intend to call, but what I've heard those other fathers say has got me all emotional-like and made me start thinking about my own dad. I've shed a lot of tears already today, because we buried him this morning. He was seventy-eight and had been failing for the last few months, so it wasn't a shock; but the tears came, because I'm sure going to miss him.

Marve: Quite a dad, huh?

Caller: Well, yeah. He was quite a dad. His life was kind of tough. He married Mom when they were both young. In ten years they had six children. One day he went to work as usual—and never came home. I guess the pressure was too great. We didn't see or hear from him for forty years. Then nine years ago somebody knocked, and when I opened the front door I saw this man on the porch looking at me and grinning. I knew as quick as I looked into his eyes that he was my dad.

Marve: Wow! Home after forty years. So what next?

Caller: Well, I just acted like he'd been away at work that day, and I asked him to come in. It was quite a shock to Susan when I called her into the room and said, "Honey, this is my dad." A few minutes later our two married children happened to drop by, because it was Susan's birthday. As the first one came in I said, "Charles, I'd like you to meet your grandfather." I did the same when the second one came in. I've never seen as many shocked expressions as I saw that night. Later I called each of my five brothers and sisters and told them that Dad had come home.

In the days that followed we learned that he was not well and could not care for himself. For the next four years he stayed with Susan and me for a while and then with his other sons and daughters. And like I say, we buried him today.

Marve: No hard feelings about his deserting you?

Caller: Oh, yeah, of course. But all that's painful water under the bridge. We had nothing to gain by having bad feelings. But by forgiving him we could gain a father. And you know, Marve, next to a mother, there just isn't anything in this world that a child of any age can have that is as wonderful as having a father. And now for the past nine years we've had a father. We came to love him with all our hearts.

Marve: Didn't you have a desire to tell him to hit the road?

Caller: Oh, no! No, no! You see, Marve, he's our father. Yeah, I would have liked to have him around in all my growing-up years. He would have come in handy on a number of occasions. Life can be tough without a father. But I'm glad he finally came home, and even though today is a sad day I still feel like having my dad come home has made me the world's happiest man.

Marve: Well, I don't know about all that. That guy has a more forgiving heart than I do. I think if that had been my father I would have told the old guy, "Hit the road, Jack." . . . Hello. You're on the air.

Caller: Come on, Marve. You think you're tough, but I'll bet you'd have done just what that guy did.

Marve: Well, I'm not sure. Who knows? My dad was always there. But that didn't seem to do me a lot of good. He and I didn't see eye to eye. To him, everything was either black or white. He had his mind made up on every issue. About the only time we talked it was a contest of wills. That's why I joined the navy when I was eighteen. I wanted to get away. I never thought I'd miss the old guy, but I did. Even now as I think of him I find myself feeling more sure of just who I am.

Caller: Is he still alive?

Marve: No, he died two years ago. And you know, they talk about life after death and I don't know much about that, but the funny thing is that each year that goes by I find myself becoming more like him. It's sort of like he still lives through me. But wait a minute! The longer this show goes, the more I feel like I'm letting my heart get in the way of my head. So, I'm gonna say less and let you happy guys do all the talking. I challenge all you guys who feel like you're the happiest man alive! . . . Go ahead, you're on.

Caller: Hey, Marve! You're confirming what I've suspected for the last year. You're not the hard guy you try to be. At heart, you're a softy.

Marve: Don't be too sure. If I was a softy, then maybe . . . Well, let's get on with it, here. Do you have a claim to happiness, or are you just calling to psychoanalyze me?

Caller: No. Well, yeah. I do. I'm not married, and I have no children and I'm free. Marve, that's happiness.

Marve: Come on, fella. When you've known marriage like I have and you've got children like I do—and then suddenly when you know you're losing all that, you can't stake any legitimate claim to happiness. Anyway, I'm not here to judge, but I'm taking you off the list of the candidates for the world's happiest man. . . . Hello.

Caller: Marve, this is Gail.

Marve: Gail, didn't you hear our rules? If you've been listening you know this is an all-male show.

Caller: I know, but don't cut me off. I called to talk about a man, so that ought to qualify me to speak.

Marve: Okay. For you, we will make an exception. Who is this man about whom you desire to speak?

Caller: Oh, Marve, he is the world's greatest man.

Marve: Oh, yeah! Who is it?

Caller: Marve, he is my husband, and he's the handsomest guy in all of Cedar Falls. He is an athlete, and tonight at dinner he was voted the number one "one-on-one" basketball player in our family. Our oldest son didn't vote for his father, but for himself. That one negative vote didn't go over well with my sweetheart, so they are out on the driveway court now settling the issue.

Marve: So you've got a hoop out there?

Caller: Yes, we do. John—he's my husband—he puts a hoop up before he plants a lawn. He loves basketball with a passion. Of course, he loves tennis nearly as much, but he can't beat me at that so he takes pride in his basketball prowess.

Marve: So you're a tennis star?

Caller: Yeah, I'm pretty good. John insists that we all do a lot of playing together, so we are all pretty good at most sports—even hopscotch.

Marve: When you find out who wins the game, let me know and I'll come down and thrash the winner. I'm from Indiana, so you know I've got the credentials.

Caller: Hey, they're coming in. I'll ask who won. My husband is smiling. He must have won.

Marve: Hey, Gail, put your son on and let me ask him.

Caller: Okay. His name is Jason.

Marve: Hey, Jason, how did you do against the old guy?

Caller: He beat me.

Marve: He beat ya?

Caller: Yeah.

Marve: Why'd you let him do that?

Caller: Well, he was the referee too, and that helped him down the stretch.

Marve: Is he a good player?

Caller: Oh, sort of. But he was mostly just lucky. But tomorrow night I'll get him.

Marve: Tomorrow? Do you play every day?

Caller: No, not usually. Just two or three nights a week.

Marve: Sounds like you and your dad spend a lot of time together. Is he a good father?

Caller: Yeah, he's the best.

Marve: The best? What makes you think so?

Caller: I dunno. He's a good man, and he's fun to be around.

Marve: Put your mom back on. . . . Sounds like your husband spends a lot of time with you and the children. Does he ever work?

Caller: Oh, yes. He was just made a vice-president at General Electric. But he's a clock watcher there. He says he works his head off while he's on the job and then hurries home to do the more important things, such as being a husband and a father.

Marve: You mean things at home are more important to him than things at work?

Caller: Well, in a way. He does well at work. But he says that if he left General Electric they'd keep going just fine without him, but if he ever left me and the children, we'd miss him forever. He has a saying behind his desk at work that says, "No other success can compensate for failure in the home." Marve, I've got to go. He's in teasing the children and they're having so much fun I need to get in there and protect them.

Marve: Hey, before you go . . . Tell him he has been drafted as a candidate for the title of the world's happiest man . . . Sounds like quite a guy. I wonder if General Electric knows that one of their VPs is a clock-watcher who considers his family more important than their big-screen TVs? How would it be to be the family "one-on-one" champ? How would it be to be any kind of champ in your own home and to have your wife feel like she was married to a . . . Anyway, we've got time for one last call. Hello. You're on.

Caller: Marve, it's Sarah.

Marve: Sarah . . . You've never called before.

Caller: Marve, please come home.

Marve: I thought that last week we decided . . . or, uh, you decided that that was it. It wasn't worth it.

Caller: I've been listening. Marve, please come home. The girls and I . . . we need you. We love you and we need you.

Marve: I, uh, I'll be there in an hour. No, Sarah, make that forty-five minutes . . . It's news time. This is Marve Levy. We have a winner. The winner is me and every father everywhere.

"Grandpa, Are You Awake?"

Grandparents, just by doing what comes naturally, have a positive influence on their adult children and grandchildren. This influence can be enhanced by proactively fulfilling the grandparenting role.

INTRODUCTION

"Grandpa. Grandpa! Grandpa! Are you awake?"

If I hadn't been, I was now. It was five-thirty in the morning in Houston, Texas. Just two days after Christmas.

As I forced open my eyes, I saw my four-year-old grandson, Kolby, standing at my side and studiously staring at me to see if there were any signs of life. Seeing his face through the dimness of the early morning light was like seeing the sun come up, and suddenly I could answer with great enthusiasm, "Yes sirree, Kolby! Your grandpa is wide awake."

"Get up, Grandpa. It's time to play."

Five minutes later I was sitting on the front room floor pushing Thomas the Tank Engine down his wooden track as Kolby, who sat at my side, drew Thomas on his Etch A Sketch. It was for moments like this that I had made the long journey from my home in Provo, Utah, to Kolby's house in Houston, Texas. It was for moments like this that I thanked the Lord for the joy and privilege of being Grandpa.

As I looked at what my grandson was drawing on the Etch A Sketch, I was intrigued by how that little machine worked and I said to Kolby, "I get to play with the Etch A Sketch next. Okay?"

"Okay, Grandpa. I'll be through in a minute. Then I'll let you have a turn. Right now you just keep pushing Thomas, okay?"

"Okay," I said with a little feeling of impatience.

As I looked at Kolby's excited expression my heart welled up with love for him, and I reached out and pulled him close to me and said, "Grandpa needs a hug from his friend named Kolby."

"Don't hug me right now, Grandpa. You made me make a line that I didn't want to make."

As he pulled away I asked him, "How come I love you so much, Kolby?"

He laughed and said, "I don't know." He then quickly added, "Maybe it is because I let you play with my toys." I smiled and thought to myself, "That is only a part of the reason. There is more to it than that. Much more." But this serious thought was not for now, so I turned and pushed Thomas the Tank Engine down the track passed Sir Topham Hatt, the railroad superintendent.

I found myself being glad that Kolby's parents were still sound asleep. We had all been up late the night before, and so they needed their rest. But the greatest reason I was glad was that I could have Kolby all to myself. And that was a bit like being in heaven without dying. The only thing that marred those golden moments was my longing to get hold of the Etch A Sketch. And maybe soon even that would happen.

It is good to be a son. It is good to be a daughter. It is good to be a father. It is good to be a mother. But the Lord saves the best until last, for the crown of life's joys comes when we become Grandma and Grandpa.

Fortunate is the family in which the children have living grandparents. Be sure as parents and grandparents to take advantage of this family asset while it lasts.

GRANDPARENTS CAN PROACTIVELY DO CERTAIN THINGS

1. **Be aware of the power of your natural and inherent position as grandparents.**

This natural and inherent love puts grandparents in position to do much to positively influence grandchildren.

While I served as president of the Missionary Training Center in Provo, it was my sad responsibility to tell several missionaries of the death of a father or mother. As you would do, I made a fervent appeal to the Lord for his help, for myself and for the grieving young missionary.

Much more often than informing them of the passing of a parent, I told missionaries of the death of a grandparent. I felt that this would be easier. But in that, I was quite wrong.

I recall the first time that I informed a missionary of this sad news. I sat with a young elder in my office to inform him that his grandfather had died. I, of course, had a great concern and was as gentle and considerate as I could be.

I said, "My dear friend, it is my sad duty to tell you that your grandfather passed away last night."

His reaction, to a slight degree, surprised me. It shouldn't have, and it did not thereafter. But it did this first time. He started to cry. A seemingly endless flow of tears fell from his eyes. I sat in silence, sensing his deep emotional distress. When his gentle sobbing had almost stopped, I softly said, "Tell me about your grandfather."

Wiping the tears away, his eyes brightened as his mind filled with the memories of his living grandfather. A smile came upon his face as he began to speak. He told me of the experiences he had shared with his grandfather. They had spent time fishing and farming and just being together. He told me of how his grandfather had so often affirmed him when he felt discouraged and unimportant. He told me of the faith of his grandfather and of the love that his grandfather and grandmother had for each other. He told me many more sacred things about the relationship that he had with his grandpa.

I asked, "Was the news of the passing of your grandfather a surprise to you? Did you know that he was sick?"

"It was not a surprise," he replied. "Grandpa had been sick for more than a year. I knew that he wouldn't be there when I returned from my mission. Mom and Dad have cared for him in our home for the past two years. He couldn't talk the last several months, but he could listen, and I used to talk to him each day when I'd come home from school or work. He got so he could hardly remember anybody, but I could tell that somehow he could remember me."

With that he began to gently sob again. But then it appeared that a quiet revelation entered his heart, and the tears of this noble elder ceased. A perceptible glow of hope lighted his countenance. He sat up straighter in his chair and said, "At least now Grandpa and Grandma will be together again."

I asked with deep respect, "Do you really believe that?"

"I know that," he said. "Grandma and Grandpa taught me that."

After this young missionary left my office, I knelt among the sweet, sacred memories of what I had just heard and felt. I prayed that the Lord would continue to comfort this young grandson of a most noble grandfather. I prayed that I would leave such a legacy.

All my grandparents had died before I was old enough to remember them. So I never had the blessing of grandparents. However, I've been told that my grandfather Durrant, just before he died, used to pull me in a wagon when I was just a small infant—too young to consciously remember. Maybe that is why when I wrote the history of my family he became my favorite ancestor. I couldn't find out much about him. His obituary said, "William Albert Durrant was not prominent in the church nor in the community." I cast the paper aside and said aloud, "Well, he was prominent to me."

It was about then when he came to me in a dream and told me that he didn't know if I was proud of him but that he sure was proud of me. I told him I was very proud of him and that I loved him because he was my grandfather.

Years ago I was pulling my two-year-old grandson Georgie in a wagon in the park. As we made our way along the asphalt path that led down the gentle hill, I quickened my pace to make the ride more fun for him. I was moving about as fast as one my age can. The path was slick with moisture but that was no problem. At the bottom, when we reached the greatest speed, the moisture had turned to ice—that was a problem. My feet suddenly slid from the path and flew over my head. I crashed to the ground, landing with my full weight on my arm and shoulder.

I was stunned. The pain and shock were so great that for a minute or two I could scarcely move, let alone get up. Finally I was able to crawl to a big rock and pull myself up and sit down at the side of the path. Little Georgie, who was an eyewitness to all of this, sat in his wagon where he knew that I was in pain. When I was finally on the rock, I watched as he got out of the wagon. He picked up my earmuffs, which were lying on the path. He walked over to where I was and handed them to me, hoping this would help. At that time he only knew how to say a few words. He looked into my eyes and in the most compassionate tone I had ever heard said three times, "Sorry Papa. Sorry Papa. Sorry Papa." Those words touched my heart so deeply that I shall never forget them. My arm was broken as were several of my ribs. But his words made everything seem almost all better.

It is impossible to describe the love that I had for him at that time, and I knew that his love for me was equal to mine for him.

Looking back on that moment I knew that one time a long time ago, my grandfather had the same kind of love for me that I had for my grandson Georgie, a love that goes beyond all understanding.

2. Know and honor the difference between the role of parents and grandparents.

The role of grandparents is one of love and affirmation, not primary care and discipline.

(Note to parents: Don't rely on the grandparents as your primary babysitters. Save them for "special-occasion tending" rather than calling on them to give such service frequently.)

Let your children raise their children. You had your turn and now it is theirs. Yours is now a secondary role of love, rather than a primary role of discipline. Of course if you are tending the grandchildren while the parents are away there will be times you will need to mete out some discipline. But when the parents are there leave the discipline to them.

Every child needs to spend some time each day or so with someone who is crazy about him or her. That is the role of grandparents.

Every child wears a sign that says, "I want to be important now." It is when no one reads that sign that the child begins to lose part of his or her wonderful inward self. Grandpa and Grandma's privilege is to read and respond to that sign every time he sees the child and to make the child feel that he or she is the most important person in the world.

3. Be with the grandchildren an appropriate amount of time.

Note to parents: Live close enough to grandparents so that your children and you can see them often. If you do live some distance away, come home as often as is possible. Too long without visits will break the bond between children and grandparents and that is a tragedy. Bringing your children in contact with their grandparents puts them in touch with their family heritage and gives them a sense of their roots.

When our daughter lived many states away she wrote to us and said, "Our children are so cute but nobody here knows that because they are not their grandparents."

Go to see your children and grandchildren as often as you can. When you do visit, always leave before they want you to so that they will always want you to return.

Give the grandkids your time. Put aside some of your golf, some of your car repairs and the things that you do in your shop. Turn the TV off and experience the miracle of the way that you feel when you go for a walk with your grandchild.

Don't get the idea that I don't know that we should live our own lives and let the kids and the grandkids live theirs. We shouldn't give up all our interests for someone else's. We deserve to have time to ourselves. I know all of that. But you and I both know that anything else, I mean everything else, is not even in the same ballpark with the importance of being with the family.

My best visit:

Once I was on business to the distant town where my daughter and her family lived. I could only stay a few hours. When it was bedtime I went to the children's room to tell them stories. Before the stories Lexie and Ben began to jump up and down on Lexie's bed. Their mother scolded them and told them to stop. So I decided to take everything into my own hands and to make everything all right. Soon I was standing on the bed beside the two little ones, and seconds later I was jumping up and down with them. Neither they nor I could stop laughing. Even though my daughter tried to act exasperated, she too gave up and joined in the fun.

4. Do quiet things with them.

If you live close by, go to a grandchild's house or have him come to your house. Then for a moment or two—or longer—sit with the child; go for a walk with him; pet the dog with her; pull him in a wagon; push her in a swing; draw pictures and color with him; look up at an airplane or a bird or a cloud with her; or read a story to him.

In any one of a million ways, show and tell each grandchild that you love him or her with a perfect love. In these brief moments you don't need to run with him, swing her around, hike steep hills, or play vigorous games. That is for young parents who still have energy to burn. A grandparent's most valuable time and effort should be the quiet times where love is more important than excitement. As we said earlier, in your moments with your grandchildren you don't need to discipline them. That is parents' work, not grandpa's and grandma's work.

A grandparent's work is to look beyond any faults that the grandchildren might have and to see only their wonderful nature and the divine potential that is really in them. Grandpa's and Grandma's role is to tell them how beautiful they are; how good they are at throwing a ball; how well they read; how much you like their piano solo; how well they color with their Crayolas; how good the snake is that they made out of Play-Doh; how much they help their mom and dad; and how much you love them.

I'm making this sound like all grandchildren are very young, but these same principles are true if they are in their teens. Grandparents' affirming words and actions when the grandchildren are teenagers might make the very difference in the direction that they choose to take their lives. Many times, when they are upset at their parents, Grandpa or Grandma, without being judgmental or interfering with parental discipline, can love them into taking the good path.

If there are two or more children in the family, a grandparent can figure out and do something that shows love to each child. Often, just one minute is all it takes. It is not enough to say, "I love all four of you kids." Somehow you have to get to each one, and in a very private way, say, "You are really getting to be a great reader. How did you learn to read so well? I'll bet that you are your teacher's favorite. You sure are a favorite of mine."

Or, go to a grandson doing his homework in his room and say, "Hey, I can tell by the way that you study that someday you'll be another Einstein. I'd better not disturb such a scholar, but I couldn't leave without telling you how proud I am to be your grandma."

Or, take a child who is just learning to talk into your arms and go outside to find a bird. I think it should be illegal for anyone except Grandpa to show a little grandchild his first bird—to point at the bird and say, "Bird. Pretty bird. Can you say bird? Oh, good, you said bird. Grandpa and you love the bird, the pretty bird."

Or, hold a little child and say, "I wish that I could take you home. We'd play. Then we would eat ice cream and then we would go to the park, and then we'd eat hot dogs and potato chips and olives. We'd have so much fun! Grandpa loves you, but you'd better stay here, or your mommy and daddy would cry and cry and cry because they would miss you so much. For they love you just like I do."

5. Affirming and counseling them.

Your primary duty is to love, love, and love the grandchildren. If you do so, they will always remember with ever-increasing fondness the times they spent with grandmother and grandfather.

One of the greatest men I have ever known was Ernest Eberhard. He was a teacher of teachers. He was my teacher. He was the curriculum director and teacher trainer for the Church Educational System. The material he prepared and the stirring talks he gave to teachers ultimately led to his being awarded an honorary doctorate degree at Brigham Young University. Because he knew I loved and admired him so much it was his request in his older years that I speak at his funeral.

I sat on the stand at these services. From this vantage point I was able to look into the faces of his family members as they came in and took their seats in front. His wife, who is like an angel, looked peaceful as she entered. The four children's eyes were red from much crying but were now composed. But the teenage grandchildren seemed unable to bear the pain of the loss of their grandfather. He had been their friend and confidant. He had been their cheerleader and counselor.

When it was time for me to talk I couldn't focus on my prepared remarks about Ernest's greatness as leader in his profession. All that was pushed aside in my heart by his role as husband, father, and most of all, grandfather.

That moment, seeing and feeling the tears of these grandchildren revealed to me again the great bond of love that ties together the hearts of a grandparent and the grandchildren.

I wrote the following letter to a grandson:

15 January 2000

Dear Grandson,

I know of the recent problem that you have had. So I want to write you a letter of encouragement.

When we are young we often do things that can really be considered dumb things. And then we become aware that what we have done is really dumb. When we realize that, then we have a great choice to make. The choice is, "Now that I have done a dumb thing, am I going to keep going down that road to arrive at pure stupidity? Or am I going to turn around and go a new direction— a wise direction that will lead me to be all that I can be?"

The police or a judge can make you do some things They can even punish you by making you go to jail. But in the privacy of your own life you can lie to them and do things in secret.

Your parents can't make you change. Oh, they can force you to do a few good things, but in the privacy of your own life you can do what you want and they can't get you to do otherwise. Heavenly Father and Jesus Christ can teach you and make you feel guilty in your heart. But they can't and won't take from you your agency to do whatever you desire to do.

The only one who can get you to change is you yourself. Your change cannot be imposed upon you from the outside. Your change must come from within. And I know such a change will come. I know that in your heart you desire to change and to do good. I know that because I know who you are. You come from two great families. You have part of all of you ancestry in your heart. There is a part of me inside you. I'm far from perfect but I sure have a desire to be a good person. Because of that part of me that is in you I have in my heart a deep love for you. I've loved you ever since you were a little baby. You have always been so good, so courteous and so kind to me. So it is no wonder when I learned of the dumb things you did, it broke my heart. It made me go to

Heavenly Father and plead with him to help you to find some new friends to get some new habits. To wake up and do your school work. To attend to your church duties. Praying for you is all I can do. You can do whatever you want and I'll never quit loving you, but I'm afraid that if you don't change your course you will never be able to truly like yourself.

Take your feeling to the Lord in prayer. Kneel down and tell your Heavenly Father how you feel. Ask him to help you. Read a page or two of the Book of Mormon every day. Go to church not because you feel as though you have to. Go because you want to, because you love the Lord. Religion is the way to gain the strength to do the things that will lead you to a life of joy and not misery. You need to prepare for college, to prepare for marriage and fatherhood. You may or may not desire to serve a mission. That is not the important thing—the important thing is to be a man of honor and goodness.

From now on I want to go out to lunch with you each Tuesday. As we sit in our favorite restaurant I'll ask you how you are doing. Let's go there each week until we have tried every item on the menu. You can order for me and get my drink and take care of me. I love you, my dear grandson. My prayers are with you always.

Sincerely, Grandpa George

6. Phone them often.

Sometimes when Marilyn and I are at home together, certain of our grandchildren come into my mind and heart. I get up, go to the phone, and call them. I say something such as, "Hello, this is Grandpa George."

Then I talk to little four-year-old Eliza by asking, "What are you doing?" She answers. I tell her that I love her. Then I say, "I wish I was at your house so that we could play and eat ice cream." And then I'm really out of ideas. So I ask to talk to little Annie. I ask Annie the same things, and then I ask to talk to their mom or their dad. After thirty seconds of talking to Mom or Dad, I can't think of anything else to say. I'm just not good at talking on the phone. But then I get to the real purpose of my call. I say to the parent that I'm talking to, "Grandma wants to talk to you." I give her the phone and she talks to them and talks to them and talks to them. On and on it goes. She really is a master at talking on the phone.

The longer the conversation goes the more I like it, because I feel that if they can talk to Grandma Marilyn, then all will be well with this little family who mean so much to me. When she finally hangs up, I go to her and ask, "What did they say?"

She replies, "Why are you asking me? You talked to them."

I reply, "But I didn't know what to say. You know I can't talk on the phone. Tell me what they said to you." Then she gives me a report on all that they said. As she does so, I thrill at her every word.

It seems as if everything is like that. I'm good at the mountain peaks of grandparenting, but she covers the matters which have great depth. The best thing that I do as Grandpa is to help the grandkids and their parents to come in frequent contact with Grandma.

7. Tell them stories of the olden days.

For a Christmas present one year I used a tape recorder and recorded every olden-day story that I could remember. I told story after story of little things that had happened to me. One story led to the memory of another. I gave each grandchild a tape of those stories, and they often listen to them when they go to bed. My stories put them right off to sleep.

Telling your personal olden-day stories is a good way to leave a bit of your history to your grandchildren. You should do that, you know. We are all encouraged to write our personal histories. I'm trying to get a law passed making it a felony for any grandpa and grandma to die before they have written their personal history or at least told thirty-seven stories on tape about when they were little kids.

This is a story I have told my grandchildren:

As a teenager I really wanted a Studebaker (a car that looked the same in the front and back) so bad that it was always on my mind. I could see myself driving it. All the girls in town would want to ride in it with me, and I would be the most popular boy in the whole big town of American Fork. I could see myself, as plain as day, driving my Studebaker up the hill towards American Fork High School. I'd whiz past all the other young people who were walking to school. All of them would wish that I would stop and give them a ride. The two prettiest girls in town would see me going by, and one of them would say to the other, "There goes old George."

The other one would reply, "How do you know he is going? He might be coming. You can't tell in a Studebaker."

I never did get that fancy car but I didn't mind, because it was more fun to have a Studebaker in my mind than it was to have one in my garage.

Another story:

I was in the army, but I was never in a battle. When we'd be marching I'd try very hard to not make any mistakes, because we had a real mean sergeant. If you made a mistake while you were marching and went right when you were supposed to go left, he would call you bad names. I didn't want to be called bad names by the mean sergeant.

Each night when I'd pray, I'd say, "Heavenly Father, please help me to march good so that the mean sergeant won't get angry and call me those bad names that he calls the other soldiers."

Then one Saturday we were standing in formation in front of our barracks, waiting to be dismissed. I was happy that we would have the afternoon off, and I was thinking about that instead of about marching. The mean sergeant shouted, "Left face!"

I got confused and did a right face, and that made it so everyone else was facing away from the mean sergeant, but I was standing face-to-face with him.

My heart pounded with fear, for now I knew that the mean sergeant would call me bad names, just like he called all of the other soldiers bad names when they made mistakes.

But as I looked into the mean sergeant's eyes, he couldn't seem to even talk. Then in a really soft voice he said, "Private Durrant, turn around." Then he said, "Company dismissed!"

Everybody shouted with happiness and ran toward the barracks. But instead of running and shouting, I quietly and slowly walked away. I was very happy that Heavenly Father made it so that the mean sergeant could not call me bad names.

I learned that if you pray, Heavenly Father will protect you against things like the words of the mean sergeant. That is why I hope all of my grandchildren and their children will always say their prayers every night and every morning.

Leave for your grandchildren stories about your life, your dreams, your faith, and your love. You don't have to brag. Some of us don't have much to brag about. But if they know that you spilled your soup once at school lunch and they made you clean it up while all the other students watched and that you didn't get many valentines and that you didn't really have a Studebaker and that the mean sergeant couldn't say bad things about you because you prayed, then you have given your grandchildren your greatest gift—not anything you had, but everything you are.

8. Be an example to them.

With great blessings come great responsibilities. It is not enough just to be called Grandpa. We must in very deed be Grandpa. We must truly be awake.

It is the responsibility of you as Grandpa to stand on holy ground as a worthy high priest, and to prayerfully and diligently lift the grandchildren to that ground. You, as a grandpa, do not have to be perfect, but you need to want to be. And if that is your desire, the Lord will lift you up, and in the eyes of your grandchildren you will be perfect. Be a fine old high priest.

9. Pray for them.

I love to go walking each day. I go to a beautiful park. There is a small stream there and many tall trees. Under the trees I say a brief prayer in which I talk to the Lord about certain members of my family who seem to have urgent needs. At least once each week in that beautiful place I say a special family prayer. At that time I mention each of my children and grandchildren and ask a special and individual blessing that I feel that each one needs at the time. As I mention each one by name, I feel a real closeness to him or her. It takes a while and I do it silently. The great body of the prayers which Marilyn and I say each night and morning centers on our children and theirs.

10. Be a patriarch to them.

As one settles into his grandfather years, the word "patriarch" takes on greater meaning.

My dictionary says of the word patriarch: "The father or head of a family like Abraham, Isaac and Jacob. Any very old or dignified man. A high dignitary who has the right to invoke and pronounce blessings."

You may not feel that you are dignified, but in our own way

you and I really are quite dignified, if we overlook some of our undignified ways.

The last part of what my dictionary said is what really impressed me: "A high dignitary who has the right to invoke and pronounce blessings."

I'm sure that you, like me, are not a high dignitary out in the city or even in the neighborhood. But in our own families we are quite high dignitaries.But now I want to go to the last part of that which my dictionary said: "The right to invoke and pronounce blessings."

One day, I began to think of my children and my grandchildren. I decided that I would like to go to their homes and give each of them a blessing. It wouldn't be a Patriarchal Blessing, because I am not a Patriarch. It would instead be a patriarchal blessing, because I am a patriarch.

So, I wrote each family a letter telling them that I would like to come to their home on a special night and give them each a blessing.

The first to respond were Devin and Julie. On the appointed night, when Marilyn and I arrived, we were greeted in the high dignitary fashion to which we have become accustomed. Devin seemed more sober than usual. He shook hands with me and called me "Father." When he called me "Father," I sensed that he knew the full significance of what was about to happen. Dads and grandpas can do certain things, but other things are reserved for fathers and grandfathers. It is by being a good dad and grandpa that we earn the right to, at times, be called "Father" or "Grandfather."

After visiting for a while the sacred time for the blessing had come.

I decided to start with the youngest child and go to the oldest. Ryan was first, and although he was only three years old he seemed to sense what was happening. Then Heather, then Laura, then

Emily (my little disciple), then mother Julie, who longed to have another baby but who had not been able to conceive (we made a special mention of that in her blessing), and then father Devin. As Devin stood up following his blessing, he was crying. He was deeply touched. Then Devin gave his mother a blessing, and then he gave me one. The things that he said in my blessing gave me much hope for the future.

We ate a piece of cake, but the mood in the home was more like the temple than it had ever been before.

My oldest son, Matthew, and his family live in Salt Lake City, and we don't get there as often as I would like. A phone call was made to arrange the time. When we arrived, it was late Sunday afternoon and we rang the doorbell the way that high dignitaries do. The children and the little white dog ran to the door, shouting and barking. We were greeted with uncontrolled glee. It was difficult to tell who was happiest—us or the children. Or maybe it was Jackie, the mother. She always makes us feel as though, next to her husband and her parents, we are the greatest people upon the face of the earth.

She took our coats and invited me to sit down. "What can I get you to eat?" she asked.

We assured her that anything would be fine. But she said, "No, you tell me what you want, and whatever it is, I'll make it for you."

She had made some soup, and it was just right. As we sat there eating with that family it was again just like being in heaven. I looked at Jacob, the fourteen-year-old computer whiz. (You have a grandchild who is a computer whiz—every grandfather does.) His quiet smile melted my heart. He has such respect for every good thing and for all people, including us, his grandparents.

I looked at twelve-year-old Andrea, the tennis player, who seemed, as usual, to be so royal. I turned my gaze to Jessica, the one whose talent is so big that it hardly fits into her young body.

I smiled at Ellie, who could get a patent on her pure version of love. I looked at three-year-old Mattie, the one who knows only joy, and last of all I looked at pretty little Kelsey.

A while later Matthew asked, "Father, would you now be willing to give us each blessings tonight as you promised us in your letter that you would?"

Before we began the blessings, I told the children about the government that we would have in heaven when we all got there. I said, "There won't be any mayors or governors or presidents in heaven. The government there will be a family government. In heaven we will have a patriarchal government. You will look to your father there as your respected patriarch. You will also look to your grandfather as a patriarchal leader. Each of you will govern yourself there, but we will be a family in heaven just at we are here, and that will be our government. So now as I give you a blessing it will be a blessing from one of your patriarchs, your grandfather."

Kelsey was first to receive her blessing. She wasn't overly impressed, because her father was holding her and my hands were on her head and she wondered what was going on. So her blessing was short.

Next came Mattie. His real name is Matthew George Durrant. I wanted him to be named George, after me, but the best I could get was for that to be his middle name. As I blessed him, I softly said his first name, "Matthew." Then I said in a loud voice, "George." Then I added in a normal voice, "Durrant." He too was a bit restless and received a short but very meaningful blessing.

When I in turn blessed Ellie, Jessica, and Andrea, the blessings grew longer. A spirit of peace and love came into each of our hearts.

Finally it was time for Jacob's blessing. My oldest grandchild. I began his blessing the same way that I had begun all the others. I called him by name and then said, "As your grandfather I seal upon you all the blessings that your father has given to you as you have progressed through your life.

"And now, I add a special blessing to those blessings. As your grandfather, I will now listen to our Heavenly Father and tell you all the thoughts that come into my heart about your life and your eternal destiny."

Thought after thought poured into my heart, and I related them to this dear young man. I could feel the great love that our Heavenly Father has for him. As I felt these things I could scarcely speak. It was as if we were all in the very halls of heaven.

Then it was my privilege to give my dear daughter Jackie a blessing. It was very much a blessing of love and appreciation for her deep devotion to my son and to my grandchildren. In the blessing, more than at any other time, I was able to tell her how much I love her.

And finally my beloved son, Matthew Burnham Durrant, sat in the chair and received, as he had so often, a blessing at the hands of his father.

All the children wanted to have grandpa receive a blessing, and so my son Matt gave me a blessing. After the blessings were over we sat and talked. Little Kelsey sat on my lap and I was happy.

We'll visit this family again. But never again will our visit be like the night that I gave them each a grandfather's blessing—blessings that will be answered to the very letter.

That night I knelt down and thanked Heavenly Father for the joy of being a patriarch, a high dignitary, a grandpa, with the power to invoke and pronounce blessings upon his family.

11. Have a family dream and make it come true.

My favorite family story, and the model after which I have fashioned my dream of the future of my family, came to me from a man I met in a distant state.

At the time I had this experience I was a young father. I was on a speaking tour, and I stayed in this man's home. That night when all the others in the family had gone to bed, this father and I were conversing in a very heart-to-heart manner. On that unforgettable evening, he told me this story:

Two months ago we had a most amazing thing happen in our family. For years we had wanted to go to Disneyland. This was the year we were to go. We had saved for this trip for several months. Now we had the money and the vacation time to go. Three weeks before we were to depart, we were sitting at the dinner table. There was a feeling of real gloom in our home. I tried to cheer everybody up, but I could not. We ate in that silence that sometimes falls upon families.

Finally my oldest son, seventeen years old, asked, "Why do we have to go to Disneyland?"

I about fell off my chair. Almost in anger, I said, "Now, just what do you mean by that? Have you and your friends planned something? You are getting so that nothing in the family is as important as being with your friends."

"No, it's not that," he said softly.

Again silence returned. Then my daughter said, "I know what Jed means, and I don't want to go to Disneyland either."

I was shocked. We had planned this trip for years.

I almost shouted as I said in a commanding voice, "Well, whether you want to or not, we are all going to Disneyland."

My wife put her hand gently on my hand and said, "Your brother phoned today and told us his children really felt bad that we were going to miss Kenley Creek this year to go to Disneyland, and I think that is what is troubling the children."

Then, almost in chorus, the children said, "We want to see our cousins. That is why we don't want to go to Disneyland."

I said, "Hey, look, I want to see the family, too. But I only get so much vacation time, and we all decided it would be Disneyland.

The family goes to Kenley Creek every year. We went there last year, and we'll go there next year, but this year we decided on Disneyland. Of course, if you all want to change the plans, well . . . I'd sooner see my brothers and sisters. But I thought this time we would do what you wanted to do."

My oldest son, who is known for his tough-guy attitude, seemed near tears as he asked, "Can we change, Dad?"

So we changed plans. I phoned my brother, and while we were talking I told him that we had decided to go to Kenley Creek. I could hear him shouting to his children, "Your cousins are coming to Kenley Creek!"

Our children were happy again.

Then this father told me the story of Kenley Creek. He said:

When my father and mother were young we did not have much money. We couldn't go on vacation to any place that cost a lot. So every year Mom and Dad would pack the wooden grub box with all kinds of food. We'd tie the old canvas tent to the top of the 1941 Ford. All us children would pile in like sardines in a can and off we would go to the mountains and to Kenley Creek.

We did that every year. Finally my older brother got married. His wife was sort of a fancy, rich girl. She had been all over the country on vacations. We didn't think that she would go with us to Kenley Creek, but she did and she had the time of her life.

One by one we all got married, and every summer at a certain time we would all come home and drive up to Kenley Creek.

The year after Dad died, we wondered if we should go. But Mom said that Dad would want us to go and that he'd be there with us. And so we all went.

As the years passed, each of us brothers and sisters had children of our own. My brother could play the accordion, and each night under the moonlight of the Kenley Creek sky he played polkas and all the kids would dance with their cousins.

Finally Mom died. But every year at Kenley Creek, in the

quiet of the mountain evening, it seemed like Mom and Dad would come back and sit by the campfire with all of us. With the eyes of our hearts we could see them smile as they watched the grandkids dance and eat the watermelon that had been cooled by the cold waters of the stream. We brothers and sisters would talk of the times gone by, and Mom and Dad would just listen.

We all were a family, and we loved each other more and more as the years passed by.

When we decided to go to Disneyland, I guess I just didn't know how much these family ties meant to the children. We knew how much it meant to us but not to them.

So we changed our mind and went to Kenley Creek. We did so because being with our family meant more than all the Disneylands in the world.

So the Kenley Creek model became symbolic to me of that which I wanted most in my life. I just wanted a family wherein all the family members liked each other. A family where each member wanted to come home. A family that liked to be together.

12. Schedule and carry out family activities.

This desire to strengthen family ties seems to intensify as we become more mature in years. Perhaps that is why Marilyn and I recently wrote this letter to our children and grandchildren:

Dear Family,

Please carefully consider the following dream that we as grandparents have tried to put on paper. Study it with your children; revise it so that you feel you can really support it. Send us your thoughts on how it can be improved. We feel that if we all share the same dream, it will surely come true. When we all have agreed, we will call it "Our Family Dream."

This, then, is that dream:

We will love all other family members, and we will do the things that people who love each other do. Namely:

— We will visit each other as often as possible.

— We will try to attend the yearly family activities.

— We will pray for each other.

— We will rejoice in the success of other family members.

— We will be emotionally and spiritually supportive of one another.

— We will each have personal integrity and bring honor to the family.

— We, when we speak of other family members, will do so as if they were present.

To help our dream come true, we will do things together. Whenever possible all family members will attend the following five annual family activities:

1. Overnight Family Campout

2. Overnight Olympic Games, Genealogical Report, and Talent Show

3. Backyard of Fire: This will be held at the old family home. It will include dinner and fireworks and Warren's famous marching music. This date will be on the evening of the Fourth of July.

4. Christmas Party: This will be held at various places to be determined each year. The date will also be chosen each year.

5. Saturday Family Temple Session

Note: If any of the children live away from Utah, they will come home when they can to be at these events, and Grandma and Grandpa will visit them twice each year.

CONCLUSION

THE THREE GENERATION FAMILY

Generally our time on earth spans three generations—grandparents, parents, and children. Of course there are exceptions, because sometimes children grow up without grandparents. And on the other hand, there is often a fourth generation in a family. Those in this generation are called great-grandparents. To me, it is sad when children do not have the blessing of living grandparents. Children don't miss grandparents whom they never knew, because that is not the way things are.

But when they do have grandparents it is such an added blessing to family life. And when they have great-grandparents it is a most sacred blessing. Sometimes I think that it is a great mistake for parents to move to places where they and the children are at a great distance from the grandparents. The opportunities for employment should not outweigh the blessings of intergenerational love and togetherness.

When I think of the three-generation family, I think of myself, the grandfather; Devin, the father; and little Ryan, the grandson. I could think of other such models in my family, but something special happened with Ryan, Devin, and me. You see, I was born on October 20, 1931. Devin was born on October 20, 1960. And Ryan was born on October 20, 1991. Can you imagine the thrill that came to me when my son was born on my birthday? Then came the added joy when, almost unbelievably, on my birthday, and on my son Devin's birthday, I received word that Devin's wife, Julie, was in the hospital in Orem and had just given birth to a little son.

There is something indefinably wonderful about the three-generation family. Whenever such families gather or write or phone or speak of each other, we hear the glorious titles: son, daughter, brother, sister, mother, father, uncle, aunt, cousin, and the most honored of all the titles—grandfather and grandmother, grandma and grandpa. All of these titles, and the people who bear them, when added together equal the most heart-touching of all titles—the title family.

The interrelationship of all these people is centered in the dearest of all the heart's places—the place that we call home. Home and family, coupled together, are the essence of happiness, the hope of the world, and the binding hope of the eternal future.

The best thing you can leave your grandchildren

It would be nice to leave your children an inheritance of a million dollars so that they could all go to college and on missions and maybe even have a Studebaker, but far better than that, leave your grandchildren stories about your life and your dreams and your faith and your love.

Being a grandparent is the best season of life, so let's all us grandparents step up and bless the lives of our dear grandchildren.

Oh, how I wish every child could have a grandpa and grandma who would do the things that I have just described! I wish I could do as well as I have made it sound. But sometimes I'm too tired or I have too much else to do, and I don't do as well as a grandpa ought to do. But from now on I'll try to do better.

How about you?

ABOUT THE AUTHOR

George Durrant was born and raised in American Fork, Utah. He has served in many capacities with the LDS Church Educational System. For several years he was the director of Priesthood Genealogy for the Church.

He served for three years as president of the Missionary Training Center in Provo, Utah, and he has taught religion at Brigham Young University.

He is the author of more than 20 books, including the bestselling *A Touch of Christmas.* He has also co-authored a book with his son Devin entitled *Raising an All-American.*

He is married to the former Marilyn Burnham. They are the parents of eight children.